DOES THIS TASTE FUNNY?

A Half-Baked Look at Food and Foodies

ISBN-13: 978-1477484166

ISBN-10: 1477484167

To everyone who believed I could do this, and to everyone who helped me survive until I did.

AS-L, BH, BS, CC, CH, CO, CT, CW, DB, DC, DD, DF, DG, DJ, DM, DM, DM, DO, DR, DRT, EH, EJ, FE, FH, FM, GH, GWB, IP, JB, JJ, JLS, JS, JT-S, JZL, KB, KK, KM, KS, LD, LK, LM, LW, ME, MF, MF, MO'L, MP, MS, MT, MW, OS, PE, RB, RD, SAS, SD, SR, SS, TO, VH, VR,

and especially, GEB

contents

contents

Cooking Through the Crazy

When I think about my mom's cooking, the first thing that comes to mind is squash. I remember squash, because we grew it in the back yard. Sadly, that meant that every meal I had at home for eighteen years had some squash-related element.

Banana squash, acorn squash, zucchini. Every single meal. I don't even remember if I liked it, but I do know I haven't eaten a lot of squash in the last thirty-four years.

My other evocative memory of food and childhood is of my mom making what's known in Danish as 'frikadeller,' which sounds so much more exotic than 'cheap ground beef and some onion in *Campbell's Cream of Mushroom* gravy.'

I can still see myself standing by my mother's side, stealing chunks of raw ground beef, adding some salt, and chowing down. It was a more innocent time, and *E. coli* was the farthest thing from my mind.

I think like most Americans, the first thing I ever 'cooked' by myself was ramen noodles, in college. Strange concept, ramen noodles.

Not the noodles themselves, but the fact that the package contains the noodles and something called, in Orwellian style, a 'flavor packet.' I have since learned that some foods actually have flavors *already built in*, as opposed to requiring you to *add* 'flavor.'

The first time I ever *read* about food (not including menus) was about fifteen years ago. It was a time when the President had been impeached, NASA had lost a spaceship, and the country was reeling from the divorce of Pamela Anderson and Tommy Lee.

I worked at a bookstore in California, and I was randomly assigned the food section. Although 'worked' is a stretch, since once the books were shelved and their spines faced out, there wasn't much to do, unless there was a customer.

It felt like I was getting paid eight bucks an hour to read! I'm don't know if there were other things I was *supposed* to be doing, but I know did a lot of reading.

The store was promoting Thomas Keller's 'French Laundry Cookbook,' and it didn't look at all like what I thought cookbooks should look like.

From the austere white-on-white cover, to the ridiculously close-up pictures of food that looked like sculpture, to chapter titles like "The Law of Diminishing Returns" and "The Importance of Hollandaise," it was clear that this was not 'The Joy of Cooking.'

I didn't even know hollandaise sauce *had* importance! This book was like a portal into some weird, mystical world. I felt like a fourteen-year-old boy discovering Tolkien's world for the first time.

Who knew you could infuse something with white truffle oil? Who knew there was white truffle oil?

As sucked in as I was by this alternate universe, I didn't suddenly become a foodie. For most of my adult life, 'cooking' involved a can and a can opener.

I was fascinated by the *idea* of cooking, but for years, I never *cooked* anything more sophisticated than an omelet. I defrosted a lot of things. I heated a lot of things. But *cooking*, with different ingredients and...more than one pan? Not a lot. I had to ask a friend to teach me how to hard-boil eggs.

Around the time I turned fifty, I taught myself how to cook. Now, a couple years later, I'm eating home cooking almost every night.

At first, I had no idea *why* I was suddenly makin' with the mirepoix, and it was months before I figured it out. Since you asked, I started cooking to avoid going insane.

I had spent years kicking around the fringes of showbiz as a comedian, with just enough success during the standup boom to keep trying.

But years of trying to eke out a Bohemian life had ground me down, and I started to, in psychiatric parlance, lose it.

I was diagnosed with 'generalized anxiety disorder.' 'Generalized.' Yeah, thanks for narrowing it down for me, doc. "Mister Dane, it would seem that you're anxious about some things just—in general."

Well, vague though it was, at least I had proof of what I already knew.

So while I was working through my breakdown, I was also trying to live as cheaply as possible, and I figured making my own food would save a few bucks. I dabbled a little.

Then I started noticing recipes online, and buying kitchen doodads at the thrift store. Soon, I was recording episodes of 'Top Chef.'

My newfound love of the kitchen saved me some money, sure, but more importantly, it gave me something to do with my hands, and something with which to occupy my (then) unhinged mind. I had stumbled upon the perfect activity to distract me from my demons.

It's harder to worry about your long-term drama when you have a pot that's boiling over right now. Cooking is so tangible, and so very 'in the moment' Doing it allows me to get out of my head, plain and simple.

Now, if I'm stressed, I cook something. If I'm depressed, I cook something. If I'm angry, I cook things that involve a lot of chopping. You can release a lot of rage if you cut up enough carrots.

And, I figured, if I'm going to be fumbling around, making a mess of the kitchen anyway, I might as well write about it.

Unfortunately, if you add lack of experience to my inherent clumsiness and throw in the occasional panic attack, my resume didn't exactly scream 'food writer.'

I was truly starting from scratch, and all I had to guide me is a handful of old cookbooks. Well, some old cookbooks and the internet.

I like to think I put the guesswork back *into* cooking. Guessing, improvising, experimenting, and frequently making a hellish mess of my kitchen. I've burnt, undercooked, and over-seasoned a lot of food just in the last year.

If you're a food snob, this book probably isn't for you. Since I spend a lot of time mocking food snobs. Because they're ridiculous.

No matter how elaborate the prep or the presentation, we're ultimately just talking about food here. Which brings me to meatloaf muffins.

I spent several days dithering about a name for my website. I tried every variation and combination of words related to 'food' and 'humor.' I knew I was running out of ideas when I looked into the availability of 'eatyourcomedy.com' (that's available, by the way).

In a delirious moment, I almost called my site "*rustyskillet.com,*" and thought about creating a cartoon mascot *named* 'Rusty Skillet,' until I realized that sounds like the name of a buffet joint in a strip mall. Oh, and I also briefly considered 'Food Pimpin.'

Then I remembered my first successful attempt at 'real' cooking—it was *meatloaf muffins.* Granted, it came about because I *didn't* have something I needed, but accident and necessity have always been a part of my cooking process. And burn ointment.

One day, I was at the market and I bought a pre-made, pre-packaged meatloaf. This was something even *I* could cook. Just take the meatloaf out of the package, put it in a 350 degree oven for 45 minutes and *voila!* Comfort food.

Unfortunately, when I got home, I realized I didn't have one of those loaf-shaped bread baking thingies. All I had was (and a lot of my cooking stories will start with the phrase 'all I had was') a muffin pan.

But then inspiration hit me. What if I simply took muffin-sized pieces of the meatloaf and put **those** in the muffin pan? I'm a kitchen savant! I should enroll in Le Cordon Bleu!

I knew I had stumbled onto something special – I pictured Gordon Ramsey making my dish a challenge on Hell's Kitchen:

> "Come on, you donkeys! I don't believe you're doing this to me! These are crap -- where are my meatloaf muffins!"

Flush with the excitement of creation, I put the pan in the oven and waited for Meatloaf Muffins (which sounds like a villain from a Dick Tracy story).

I decided to 'google' the phrase 'meatloaf muffins,' just to see if anyone else had stumbled upon my creation. My search revealed 89,700 hits for "meatloaf muffins." I was crestfallen.

I had allowed myself to believe, for a few shining moments, that I had invented a new food item. Instead, I found Mexican Meatloaf Muffins, Italian Meatloaf Muffins, and I think there was actually a link to a page about how cliché meatloaf muffins are.

Reminds me of that one time I was really stoned. I had a bag of pretzels in one hand and a bag of chocolates in the other, and I thought – they should make chocolate-covered pretzels! Turns out, they do, but that's not the point. The point is, I wish I had some chocolate-covered pretzels right now.

C'est la vie. I *wasn't* the first person to 'muffinize' meatloaf. But I thought of it on my own, dammit, and for purely sentimental reasons, I plunked down ten bucks to buy a little piece of cyberspace that I call 'meatloafmuffins.com.'

On a deeper level, 'meatloaf muffins' may in fact be *the perfect food*. I don't want to get too technical, but I'll try to explain why:

1) They taste like *meatloaf*
2) They're shaped like *muffins*

What more could you possibly want from food? Besides, I'm living proof that meatloaf muffins are good for your mental health.

Where's My Other Whisk?

One day, I had a thought I had never had before. I thought, "I wonder where my other whisk is."

Now, I've lived most of my adult life without so much as *one* whisk, but now that I'm teaching myself to cook, a lot of strange thoughts cross my mind. And since one of my whisks was in the sink, I needed the other one.

When I first started my cooking adventure, I didn't have many tools, and some friends helped me out with donations.

Mostly, I got a lot of utensils. I could have used a basic cookbook (since I didn't really know how to *cook*), but I sure do have a lot of plastic things with handles.

If you need something stirred, or scooped, I guess I'm your guy. Oh, and I have a tube thingie with edges, that I think is used for...making things into a tube shape.

Ahh, so many utensils, so little time. See, in addition to my other challenges, I have a touch of the OCD, so my problem wasn't not knowing what these things all do so much as how to organize the drawer.

Seriously, the handles of my pans are all at the same angle in the cupboard. And my salad dressings are arranged alphabetically by country. French, Italian, Russian, Spanish . . .

I was also given a Crock Pot (capitalized, so you know this is actually 'the original slow cooker'), and a George Foreman Lean Mean Cooking Machine.

In addition, someone gave me some sort of mystical electrical device that apparently conjures up omelets. Or empanadas. I'm not sure. I'll just keep putting things into it until I figure out its purpose.

One friend gave me a bunch of spices. Now I may be a gourmand nouveau, but I know a little about spices. Your salt, your pepper. I've even been way out on the edge and used garlic salt! And lemon pepper!

Now I have coriander, and thyme. And sage. To be honest, I don't even know what coriander is, let alone whether I want to add it to my food.

And the only experience I've had with sage was when this roommate used to light a big stick of it on fire and wave it around the apartment to cover the smell of weed before a visit from his parents.

Although I'm in my fifties, my digestive tract is pushing seventy, so I have to be a little more careful about what I eat (in fact, there's a good chance that as you're reading this, I'm in the bathroom).

For instance, I'm very skittish when I cook meat. If the recipe says 375 degrees for 45 minutes, I tend do a little more for a little longer. My chicken might be a little dry, but I can guarantee it's salmonella-free.

I'm lucky to have a couple of friends who I can call if I have stupid questions. You know, like, "If I'm out of eggs, can I use mayonnaise in a recipe since mayonnaise is made from eggs?" *(The answer, surprisingly, is no.)*

I've always loved learning. Just the other day I learned that, even though you see flour in a lot of recipes, simply adding it to something 'as an experiment' is not a good idea, since apparently, without yeast, flour just ends up being this weird, warm powdery substance on top of the dish.

Until I started taking food more seriously, shopping was easy. The stuff nearest to the registers is better for you, right?

Now that I'm a little more connected to my food, I look at the all ingredients, and it can be very stressful.

Take something as simple as bread. I know multi-grain bread is a good thing. But how many grains exactly do I need?

Is twelve too many? Five doesn't seem like enough—what do those other seven grains have that I might want?

Maybe I'll get a good nine-grain. But wait -- this other bread has flaxseed! Do I need that?—is that one of the nine, or did they leave that one out? Shopping takes me hours.

After reading a few cookbooks, I felt I was ready to post my first recipe online. This one involved multiple steps, AND at one point I was using three of my four burners *at the same time.*

I wasn't sure what to call my creation. I decided against 'Random Cheap Food in a Pyrex Dish,' since that was a little too 'on the nose,' so I went with something that's catchy, includes a nod to my bookstore past, and honors the spirit of my ingredients.

Remainder Casserole

This dish is perfect for a chilly fall day, or for when you need to eat something but you're out of pretty much everything because you're too lazy to leave the house

Ingredients

- 1 chunk of ground beef
- 1 little bit of olive oil
- 1 big-ass white onion you meant to use before
- 1 *Band-Aid* brand adhesive bandage
- 1 bag of flour
- half a package of *Manischewitz* wide egg noodles
- some garlic powder
- a little too much celery salt
- a handful of bread crumbs
- a few globs of *Paul Newman's* Vodka Sauce
- 2 cigarettes

Instructions

First, disconnect smoke alarm. Cook noodles according to package directions. Remember you have noodles cooking.

Next, chop some of the onion into really tiny pieces. Apply bandage to cut on finger.

Throw onions into a bowl with the ground beef and the vodka sauce. Add garlic powder and too much celery salt.

Add bread crumbs. Decide you didn't need the bread crumbs. Too late. Mix by hand.

To a big hot skillet, add olive oil and ground beef mix. Sorta cook the beef, but not totally.

Light first cigarette. Your noodles are done now. You forgot about them, didn't you? Take them off the burner.

Drain noodles in colander. Place in Pyrex© dish, carefully and evenly layering them. Layer beef on top of noodles.

Now use that spoon to mix up the two layers, because you're worried the beef won't get cooked enough unless it's evenly distributed.

Scatter remaining bigger pieces of onion on top of dish.

Put away bag of flour, since you didn't actually need flour.

Place dish in 350 degree oven for at least 45 minutes.

Several minutes later, try to guess when you put it in, since you didn't check the time.

Decide you should put a foil tent over the dish, because you heard something once about using a foil tent.

Light second cigarette. Watch a couple of episodes of "The Daily Show."

Realize it's been almost an hour. Start to take dish out of oven. Immediately return dish to oven.

Find potholders. THEN take dish out of oven.

Tempting the Fates

I haven't been cooking long enough to become cocky, but occasionally I can really put it together. Like nifty wine-poached chicken breasts on a bed of perfectly fluffy couscous, with steamed broccoli florets that looked like the Platonic Ideal of broccoli.

That evening I said to The Girlfriend, "Now, I am a chef." Of course, she's used to my pronouncements from the kitchen, but they're usually along the lines of "I can't believe I spilled all of that," so this was a big deal.

For this one particular meal, everything *worked*. I did all of my prep *before* things needed to be put in the skillet, and the side dishes were done at the same time as the main course. I made enough for leftovers; I cooked something new to me (couscous); most importantly, it tasted good.

I usually decide what to make based on what's in the cupboard and *then* figure out what to do with it, but I had never improvised a dessert. Still, at this point, I was a chef, so how hard could it be?

I saw a can of kernel corn that I had been ignoring for weeks. It actually looked sad on the shelf, sitting there abandoned, continually passed over by the more popular canned green beans.

I knew what I had to do. I resolved to make a dessert. With a can of corn. I google 'corn dessert,' again wondering how people cooked before the internet, and I find something called '*El Atol de Etole*.'

What's weird, is I had just mentioned to The Girlfriend how I don't make traditional Salvadoran corn-based beverages nearly often enough.

Since I don't have a picture to show you, imagine a creamy yellow egg-noggy looking beverage. The recipe looked to be a breeze—just milk, corn, brown sugar, vanilla, cinnamon sticks and a pinch of salt.

You start by putting the corn and milk in a food processor. I only have a little one-button wannabe blender, but it works just like a grownup blender (as long as I only need to 'pulse' things).

In with the corn and milk I tossed the sugar, vanilla, salt . . . and cinnamon sticks. APPARENTLY I did something wrong, because after a few normal pulses, I suddenly heard a kind of 'ka-chonk' sound, followed by an otherworldly cry of pain from within my little blender.

Additionally, goo was shooting out of a hole in the top. A hole I had never noticed before, but which is apparently there to allow goo to shoot out.

Alright, I say, maybe the cinnamon sticks weren't supposed to go in. Maybe you can't, in fact, purée cinnamon sticks with a one-speed three-cup mini-blender from Target. I take the sticks out, and fire her up again.

This was going very badly. Put it this way: if a local news crew had been filming in my kitchen, the anchorman would have introduced the story by describing the scene as 'Cornmageddon.'

More horrific grinding sounds from within the machine, and I realize it had TRIED to purée cinnamon sticks, leaving lots of little cinnamon sticks mixed in with the goop.

Now in my defense, nothing on the machine or its packaging expressly warns *against* trying to liquefy cinnamon sticks, and nothing on the jar of cinnamon sticks said "DO NOT PLACE IN TINY MACHINES."

By this point most of my kitchen and at least one of our cats was covered in sweet, viscous corn juice, and the kitchen looked like a crime scene *("At this point, we believe the suspect leaves clues written in liquefied corn.")*.

Clearly I had offended the Cooking Gods with my hubris! Or, it was the fact I didn't really read the recipe that carefully.

Either way, after cleaning up the carnage *(cornage?)*, I looked at the recipe again. Now I see that it says "will thicken nicely on the stovetop," and I think, "Stove?" I don't remember using a stove.

Gradually, things started to become clearer. I finally figured out the cause of the fiasco! Only the *corn* and the *milk* go in the blender—the other stuff you add later!

I have to admit that the experience humbled me a little. But I learned something very important—that if I find a great recipe, I should read the entire thing, as opposed to just the first paragraph. Maybe even print a copy.

Or maybe I just need a more powerful blender.

Measuring Up

As much as I've learned about cooking in the last year, one thing is preventing me from getting to the next level.

No matter how good one of my 'dinner experiments' turns out, I'll probably never be able to make that dish again. Oh, we'll have something similar, but I never seem to be able to *recreate* my cooking successes.

I'm sure you're thinking, "Ooh, he must be an artist, like some jazz-inspired cooking phenom who improvises something brilliant, but, driven by his creative ambition, *refuses* to make the same thing twice." And I appreciate that you think that.

But no, the reason we won't be revisiting my Poached Dill Chicken Breasts in Homemade Mushroom Gravy on a bed of Garlic-Chili Potatoes with Grilled Asparagus anytime soon is two-fold:

> *1) I don't measure.*
>
> *2) I never write down what I've done.*

Consequently, I always have this inner conflict when I share my cooking—I want it to taste good, but not **so** good that I have to . . . make it again. Because I'm not sure I can!

A book of *my* recipes would need to say things like, "Cook until it looks like it did the last time, then let it sit for a while." My cookbook would be filled with units of measure like "a bunch," "just a little," and "long enough so that it all sticks together but isn't burnt on top."

I came across a recipe the other day that required me to convert everything from metric units. OK, it wouldn't have *required* it, if any of my measuring doodads had been metric.

Conceptually, I'm on board with the metric system (or as I affectionately call it, *Système international d'unités*). I just haven't had much call to use it.

When I look back on my high school years, I ask myself the questions we all ask:

"Should I have taken a foreign language?"
"Was my English teacher really that hot?"
"Why did I have to study the metric system?"

From about eighth grade on (way back in the last century), it was made very clear that this country would be changing over within just a few years.

Committees were formed, deadlines were set, transitional congressional oversight whatevers were convened;.

If I didn't get with the program, there would come a day when I wouldn't be able to cook, or shop, or even understand road signs.

Well, they missed that by a country kilometer. Like with so many forward-looking ideas, most Americans responded to the idea of metric conversion with about the same enthusiasm I would have for a new Tony Orlando album.

As a country, we collectively said, *"Nah, we're good."* I guess we were hoping to convince the majority of the civilized world to switch *back* to an antiquated, klunky system used by fading superpowers and a former empires.

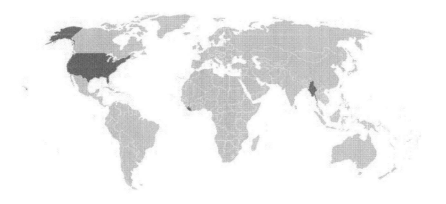

COUNTRIES WHICH HAVE *NOT* ADOPTED THE METRIC SYSTEM ARE HIGHLIGHTED

I have a theory as to why the U.S. never 'went metric.' I think the reason we stayed with our quaint 'imperial' system of measurements is the same reason half the country is abuzz every time there's a royal wedding.

My theory is that, as a nation, we all feel a little guilty about kicking England's ass in the Revolution, we're having second thoughts, and we want to become a colony again! Take us back, Mother England!

We want a figurehead leader—we want pomp and, dammit, we want it with circumstance!

We want those cool red phone booths you guys have, and double-decker buses! We're tired of trying to run the world! It's too freaking hard!

I think I would be cool with us becoming suddenly British again -- sure, I'd have to get used to cooking and eating things called 'toad in the hole' and 'bubble and squeak' and I'd have to learn a bunch of different curse words, but at least I'd have free health care.

Behind the Cooking

This seems like a good place to pull back the kitchen curtain and reveal a little of the magic. I'll take you through one meal from ingredients to ingestion, and along the way, I'll give you some insight into my 'process.'

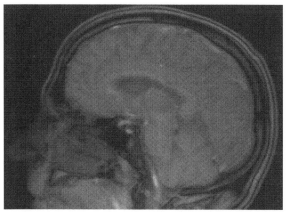

MRI OF MY BRAIN DECIDING WHAT TO COOK FOR DINNER

First of all, I always have a notepad nearby, because at any moment, I might come up with the next big thing. One night, I woke up and scrawled THREE SLIDERS SEALED PANINI-STYLE INSIDE A WIDE FRENCH ROLL. It didn't matter that we never buy French rolls, and I don't have a Panini press.

I'll ask myself questions for a jumpstart, like, "Why don't you see vanilla and peanut butter together more often?" or, "What if I shredded some macaroons, threw 'em in a pan and fried them?"

If you think something will taste good, why not try to make it? There'll be some messes along the way, and you'll throw out some food once in a while, but you'll also, sometime quite by accident, make some surprisingly good meals.

For example, one morning, with no set plan, I shredded some potatoes, chopped up some carrots, onions, garlic and celery, threw it all in my cast-iron skillet and made the most amazing vegefied hash browns (I think the key was the dollop of horseradish).

The meal we're going to analyze here is a simple meat/sauce/pasta concoction, but there was one hurdle to overcome when I made this.

Although I'm proud to be Jewish, I've never kept strictly kosher, but when I made this dish, I wasn't eating or cooking swine.

The thing is, we won a free pound of pork sausage in a contest at our grocery store, and money was tight that month. After minutes of deep spiritual questioning, I decided God wanted me to cook it.

Note: since the night I made this dish, I've relaxed my position on pork. Mostly because I remembered how much I love bacon.

About the following recipe: be sure to follow the measurements and steps precisely or . . . Well, I have no idea what might happen, but I'm not going to be responsible for it.

Capellini Con Carne Gratuito E Sugo Insolito

(Long Skinny Noodles with Free Meat and Unusual Sauce)

prep time: 10 minutes
cooking time: anywhere from 30 minutes to an hour
servings: 6 or so

Ingredients

- 1 box of angel hair pasta ('capellini')
- 1 handful of sliced mushrooms
- 1 piece of onion
- 1 stalk of celery
- 1 carrot
- A few shakes of rosemary
- The last of a small container of sage
- 1 shake of parsley
- More than I intended of cumin
- Some dill
- 1 can of organic tomato sauce
- 1 can of green beans
- Plenty of extra virgin olive oil
- A few splashes of Tabasco™ sauce
- A little kosher salt
- 1 lb. of ground pork sausage
- zero cloves of fresh garlic

What I Was Thinking

I open my cupboards for inspiration. Capellini (Italian for 'a dollar a box') is enough like spaghetti that I figure I'll just make my own red sauce.

I can cook the sausage in a skillet, and I'll just use some kosher salt to offset the whole pork thing.

Now, the onion is looking a little tired, and the mushrooms look they might turn in a couple days, so I have to use those.

And the carrot is in because, even though I've never seen either of us grab a carrot for a snack, for some reason we buy carrots every week, and I'm tired of throwing out carrots.

I know it's borderline heretical to make a pasta dish without garlic, but I was out of garlic. But it was too hot to walk to the store, so I said to myself "Screw it, I've got other spices," and "Who needs garlic anyway," and "I'll show them."

For the sausage, I grabbed parsley, sage, and rosemary, and for the next ten minutes, I had the song "Scarborough Fair" stuck in my head. (Good thing I didn't have any thyme, or I might have actually caused Simon and Garfunkel to appear in my kitchen.)

I also grabbed some dill, because it was next to the rosemary. I used cumin, because my baby loves her some cumin. Which would be a great name of an blues song.

The tomato sauce I used was organic, because The Girlfriend always buys organic, even though I'm pretty sure most of the pesticides are gone by the time the tomatoes are turned into sauce, pressure-sealed and then sautéed.

Oh, and I could have used whole mushrooms, but then I would have needed to slice them.

Instructions

 In a big pot, bring a bunch of water to a boil. Add some salt at some point in there. When the water is at a rolling boil, realize you should have prepared the vegetables. Turn off burner.

Place carrot, mushrooms, and onion into the weird little blender thing you got for your birthday. Use 'pulse' setting, as that's the only button it has. Set aside 'pulsed' veggies.

Now scoop veggies back into blender and add celery that you forgot to put in with carrot, mushrooms and onion. Set aside veggies again.

 Bring water to boil. Again. Add pasta to water. Now to duplicate my results exactly, it's very important to *forget* how quickly angel hair pasta cooks.

In a bowl, mix the sausage with the spices, including the sage, because 'adding sage' sounds like something chefs do.

Pour olive oil into a big skillet; sprinkle salt and shake the Tabasco bottle at the skillet like you're that guy in church who spreads the incense.

Heat skillet for a bit, then add sausage mix to skillet in small chunks.

Use plastic spatula to break up meat, then take partially-melted spatula out and use wooden spoon.

Start to add sauce until remember that if your meat is smothered in a red sauce you won't be able to judge the color of the meat to know if it's cooked.

Test the temperature of the meat, and then realize that since it's ground up into little pieces, you can't really use your thermometer. Try to guess when it's 'done enough'!

Turn heat down on skillet, *then* finally remember your angel hair pasta.

 Use the big pasta spoon to stir the overcooked noodles, and notice how a chunk of them have congealed into one giant super noodle. Separate this chunk.

When handle breaks off of pasta spoon, stop stirring. Melodramatically announce that you've 'ruined dinner.' Drain pasta and set aside.

Turn heat up on skillet 'just to make sure,' and add veggie mix. Stir.

Add tomato sauce and stir again. Turn heat down on skillet and cover, while you figure out what to do next.

Empty green beans into microwave safe dish and cook for a minute or so.

Drain beans, then cut beans into smaller sizes. Put beans in skillet and stir.

Pour contents of skillet over noodles. Remind yourself to get garlic. And more pork.

Ode to a Skillet

Thanks to Google and a VERY tolerant girlfriend (both of whom I love), I've been able to experiment a lot in the kitchen, and by 'experiment,' I mean 'throw things against the wall to see what sticks (sometimes literally).

Along the way, I've learned a lot. For one thing, there *is* such a thing as *too* much cumin. And since I discovered the Food Network, I frequently find myself pointing at the screen saying, "I need one of those."

To be fair, most of the time I don't in fact NEED a device that, say, shaves parsnips, or a tool designed specifically for cutting the ends off pineapples, but you get the idea.

I may not be wired like the stereotypical male in many ways, but I love gadgets as much as any of my fellow penis-bearers (have at that phrase, Auto-correct! *"Did you mean 'pall-bearers'"*?).

Seriously, how much disposable income do you have to have before you start thinking, "My life would be perfect if only my hard-boiled eggs weren't always so...egg-shaped!"

But until a very special birthday gift arrived last year, I never had the one item I needed to go from 'newbie' to foodie.' I didn't own a cast-iron skillet. Now I do, and nothing will ever be the same.

I'm sure experienced cooks are hip to the advantages of going with cast-iron, but let's review . . .

They distribute heat evenly, they last forever, and since you don't really wash them, they develop a layer of seasoning on them over time.

Another advantage to an old-school skillet is that it's the only object in the kitchen that can be effectively used to whack an intruder in the event of a home invasion.

Face it, if a burglar breaks in, you're not gonna be able to take him out with your microplane, or your breadmaker. Of course, that's assuming the burglar breaks in through the kitchen, while I happen to be cooking, but if that happens, I'll be ready.

I've only found two disadvantages to my new old-fashioned fryin' pan. One, I will quite likely need to call a neighbor to help me lift it off the burner, as it weighs more than some people's cars.

Secondly, it would have been nice if there had been SOME sort of warning label saying "IF YOU PUT THIS IN A 400 DEGREE OVEN DON'T FORGET WHEN YOU TAKE IT OUT THAT IT'S MADE OF IRON, DUMB-ASS, SO AN OVEN MITT IS A REALLY GOOD IDEA."

The friend who gave me the pan described some eight or nine-step process for properly seasoning my pan before use, but it sounded like it could involve a lot of smoke filling our apartment.

Which might be fine, except the smoke detector at our place is so freaking sensitive that it goes off if I play the *word* 'fire' in Scrabble.

Back to the aforementioned Magical Layer of Seasoning. According to the packaging, this pan was 'pre-seasoned,' so I figured I was good to go.

Thankfully, the pan came with a sheet of simple instructions to follow before use. I didn't read them, but it was nice to know they were there.

Also thankfully, I waited until after making several meals in it before I read the following at an online message board for cooking questions:

"A word of caution: Don't buy pre-seasoned cast-iron. The "pre-seasoning" is actually paint, and it can and will come off if you, you know, actually use the damn thing."

Well, thanks for that, *cookingguy1974*. Funny. You would think THE MANUFACTURER OF THE 'PRESEASONED' PAN would give you a heads-up about that. Oh well, everything tasted good, and that's what matters. Paint chips be damned.

When I was looking for things to cook with Iron Mike (yeah, I named my skillet), I turned to the web.

I had some chicken defrosted, so I searched for "cast-iron skillet" and "breasts." Oddly enough, most of the results were for Amish porn sites (*"Watch as Sister Margaret strips down to her last three layers of clothes—while she churns butter!"*).

That aside, I eventually found a recipe that looked promising and I tweaked it a bit. I browned the chicken in my own damned big, heavy, unwieldy cast-iron skillet.

Then I 'finished' the meat in the oven in that very same skillet ('finished' is cooking lingo—it means . . . 'finished').

A real old-fashioned skillet allowed me to feel connected to generations of pioneers who cooked their vittles over a crackling wood fire.

On the other hand (literally), real old-fashioned skillets can give you some wicked blisters. But there's usually a price to pay for authenticity.

Kitchen Mistakes

Since I do all the cooking for myself and The Girlfriend, she only sees the finished product, not the often clumsy steps I had to take to get there. Sometimes, however, something goes wrong in the kitchen that you don't realize until you're already eating the mistake.

I must say, up until now, my cooking screw-ups have at least been for the most part, original and creative. None of your typical mistakes, like overcooking or undercooking.

No, I do things like buy an oven thermometer and forget to put it in the oven. Turns out it's not as useful in determining the oven temperature if it's sitting on the kitchen counter.

Anyway, I'm making my soon-to-be-renowned Rustic Maple Turkey Meatballs, and I am one with my mixing bowl, using my bare hands to lovingly knead the egg into the ground turkey.

Then I blend in the garlic, onion and celery, then some hand-crushed crackers, cracked black pepper, Himalayan salt, and of course, the maple syrup. You heard me, maple freakin' syrup!

I was feeling good about our overall meatball prospects, because I recently had figured out that with meatballs, it's all about the density.

Not dense enough, and it'll just fall apart. Too dense, they can develop a gravitational field and next thing you know you have bits of your side dish orbiting each meatball.

I finish communing with the pre-ball goop (I believe that's from the French term, 'goopée'), put it in the oven and forty minutes later we're enjoying some Rustic Maple Turkey Meatballs©™. Although we really only enjoyed nine of the ten.

As I cut into my meatballs with a fork, I unexpectedly met resistance from one of them. I continued, actually sawing with the fork now, baffled by what could possibly have gone wrong with this one meatball.

Determined to solve the mystery, I pick up the meatball with my hand, and inside I see what looks like a note.

I immediately began imagining worst-case scenarios. Maybe someone working at the butcher shop is being held captive and slipped a plea for help into the ground turkey.

Or maybe The Girlfriend, in a romantic mood, wrote me a poem and hid it in a pound of raw meat?

It finally occurred to me -- I realized that in my zeal to mix everything thoroughly, I might have neglected to take all of the butcher paper off the meat. I missed one piece, about two inches square.

And that's when Inspiration slapped me in the face (because my muse is a dominatrix). I have accidentally created America's next great snack sensation—Fortune Meatballs!

Think about it—why are marginally clever, mass-produced epigrams only available inside cookies? What if you're craving a more . . . savory glimpse into your future? Fortune Meatballs!

What if, at that corporate meeting, instead of the usual cold cuts and pretzels, you could have hearty meatballs with motivational slogans tucked right inside? Fortune Meatballs!

Granted, there are some technical issues involving how best to get the fortune out of a cooked meatball, and I should probably have a lawyer look into the risk of litigation in case someone swallows their fortune (*"Warning: contains piece of paper. Do not swallow paper."*)

Maybe I could use rice paper—can you write on rice paper? I don't know. I'm more of an *idea* man.

CAN YOU GUESS WHICH MEATBALL HOLDS A SPECIAL SURPRISE?
IF YOU GUESSED SECOND ROW, THIRD MEATBALL FROM THE LEFT, THEN YOU'RE RIGHT!
CONGRATULATIONS!

I Dropped the Meatloaf

I've mentioned meatloaf before (and of course meat<u>balls</u>, which, let's be honest, are just little balls of meatloaf). In fact, maybe for my next book, I'll write EXCLUSIVELY about meatloaf.

I'll become a . . . meatloaf pundit (two words which, incidentally, have never been used in the same sentence before). I could appear on tv any time there was breaking meatloaf news (*"We're joined live by CNN's Meatloaf Correspondent"*).

Maybe it's the concept that intrigues me. Let's take some ground meat, but before we cook it, we'll throw in some bread crumbs and...get this—we'll shape it like *a loaf of bread*! It's...ironic food! My point is, I have another meatloaf story.

I was making a lamb meatloaf, and when it was nearly done, I wanted to see how it looked, and I gotta be honest. It looked like a picture from the cover of *Bon Freakin' Appetit*. Or *Meatloaf Monthly*.

It was by far the meatiest, loafiest-looking meatloaf I had ever made, all different shades of textured brown with a honey-chile glaze in a pristine white Corningware dish. Then, I dropped it.

Our language doesn't really have an adequate curse word to express what I felt as it slipped out of my hands and shattered.

I think I yelled some sort of bizarre compound word like "shitdamnfuckhell," and for a minute or two I think time stopped, as I just stood there surrounded by shards of honey-chili glazed pyroceramic glass.

One of the shards cut a gash in my foot, making me feel like the only person in the *history* of cooking to injure his foot *while* cooking.

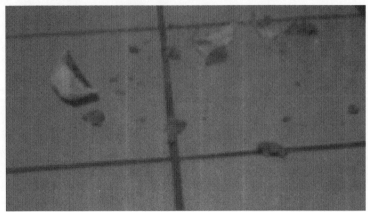

I DIDN'T HAVE THE FORESIGHT TO TAKE A PICTURE OF THE MEATLOAF BEFORE ITS DEMISE. YOU'VE SEEN MEATLOAF BEFORE. USE YOUR IMAGINATION.

But frankly, every injury I've ever had has been stupid. And although I'd like to blame the various neuro-muscular issues I'm dealing with right now, truth is, I've just always been a klutz.

I have taken some specTACular falls–I'm talkin' youtube-worthy, email the video to your coworkers ridiculous.

And if I somehow manage to walk from one place to another without tripping, I'll probably drop or spill whatever I was carrying at least once.

Jobs At Which I Would Suck

1. waiter
2. surgeon
3. juggler
4. bomb disposal guy

I just wish at least one of my scars had come from something I could brag about.

I would love to regale friends with stories of the knee I blew out playing in the state championship, or the bum hip I got serving in combat. I'd even settle for a good bar fight story to explain some of my scars. But no.

The following would be some highlights from my cavalcade of clumsy:

Apparently (I was three at the time) I thought I could do a magic trick, so I pulled the tablecloth out from under a freshly brewed pot of coffee.

A couple years later, a cousin thought it would be fun to swing me around by my arm, which promptly came out of its socket.

When I was seven, I was crawling from one box to another and dislocated my shoulder.

At eight, I tested my pocketknife to see if it was sharp, so I tested it on . . . my thumb. Our bathroom looked like a scene from C.S.I.

41

At ten years old, I jumped my bike over a hill the other kids were using in the neighborhood. Seems the other kids, though, held on to their handlebars, instead of having their bikes fly out in front of them.

In college, I was so excited that finals were over, I ran out of a building on campus, and forgot how stairs work. Broken foot, crutches.

I've broken a toe -- the SAME toe -- three times. What nimble-footed activity was I engaged in? Some sort of Riverdance thing? Nope. Walking through a doorway.

I have never been hospitalized as a result of my klutziness, and amazingly, I've never fallen down in the kitchen. Although from a safety perspective, I probably shouldn't even *be* in the kitchen, since cooking typically involves using fire, handling knives, and…carrying things.

But this story is about meatloaf, which, by the way, tasted fine. The presentation wasn't what I wanted, and we had to eat it very carefully, but it was good meatloaf.

Sometimes I Cheat

The more I cook, the more I'm willing to try something new. I'm not exactly making oxtail soup, but if dinner at home used to be Denny's, now it's a little more Applebee's. Minus the mozzarella sticks and annoyingly friendly servers.

Some people enjoy eating foods they've never tried. I've never been particularly daring. I liked escargot (drenched in butter, but maybe I just like butter), but didn't enjoy beef tongue (not so much the texture, more the concept, which seemed like sharing an inter-species French kiss).

I found both buffalo and ostrich to be disappointing. I get that they're lean, but I think meat *needs* a little fat for . . . what's the technical culinary term? Oh yeah, flavor.

Since The Girlfriend isn't very adventurous when it comes to food, my mealtime ideas sometimes require a little convincing. And sometimes I find a great idea for dinner but don't execute it very well.

I found a recipe for meatloaf (of course) that used raisins, and I hyped it pretty hard to The Girlfriend. Talked about it all afternoon. Then I forgot to put the raisins in, and ended up serving meatloaf with a *side* of raisins, while muttering that I *intentionally* deconstructed the dish.

Still, she knows that the best way for me to learn is to take risks, and most of the time the end results have been downright edible.

Sure, once in a while I'll decide to glaze a chicken breast with, say, almond butter, only to realize you can't easily *spread* almond butter on a raw chicken breast, instead creating more of a...glob than a glaze.

But I think of what I do as a kind of kitchen improv *("I need a suggestion for a vegetable you'd find in our crisper, and a type of pasta.")* And like with most improv, sometimes it clicks, and sometimes you wish you hadn't sat in the front row for it.

Last time we were at the market, we bought something neither of us had ever tried, but *had* seen on the teevee. Polenta. It's a fun word to say. Has those warm 'oh' and 'ah' sounds—it's a hearty-sounding word.

Turns out it's cornmeal mush, which sounded fine to me, but The Girlfriend seemed skeptical.

Now, don't misunderstand here -- it's not like I got all ambitious and decided to buy some cornmeal and...mush it. No, we bought polenta because IT CAME IN A FREAKIN' TUBE! ALREADY COOKED AND MUSHED!

We just figured, if all we have to do is heat it in a pan, at least we'd know our first polenta would taste like polenta should taste. However that is.

At this point, any foodie worth his or her *fleur de sel* is muttering "You should make your own polenta from scratch." Yes, homemade polenta is simple to make, *and* I'm sure it tastes marginally better, but YOU CAN BUY IT IN TUBES -- ALREADY MADE!

The only way the whole polenta process could be any simpler is if a guy *from* San Gennaro came to our place and squeezed the tube into our mouths.

To be fair let's look at both methods. I could . . .

> *"Set the water on the fire in a wide bottomed pot and add the salt.*
>
> *When it comes to a boil, add the corn meal in a very slow stream (you don't want the pot to stop boiling), stirring constantly with a wooden spoon to keep lumps from forming...*
>
> *Continue stirring, in the same direction, as the mush thickens, for about a half-hour (the longer you stir the better the polenta will be; the finished polenta should have the consistency of firm mashed potatoes), adding boiling water as necessary.*
>
> *The polenta is done when it peels easily off the sides of the pot."*

Or, I could

> *Open the tube. Heat what's inside the tube. The polenta is done when it's hot enough.*

In general, I would agree that making things from scratch is better. You're more connected to what you're eating, and it's more satisfying to taste something you worked on for hours.

There is one food item that is so ridiculously labor-intensive I almost always choose the store-bought, pre-made version. I suppose I *could*

1. thoroughly scrub and wash some potatoes
2. spend what seems like most of the evening peeling the potatoes
3. finely mince several cloves of garlic
4. boil some water
5. add the potatoes
6. wait till the potatoes are mashable
7. drain the potatoes
8. add some milk
9. add some butter
10. add the garlic
11. mash the potatoes

Or, I could just buy some garlic mashed potatoes. Yes, it might be considered cheating. I know I'm violating a sacred trust here, but at the end of the day this should be a private matter between me and my potatoes.

Footnote: In simple terms, I realized that polenta is basically Italian grits, and while I don't normally enjoy 'gritty' food ("Mmm, that's nice and gritty"), I enjoyed it. The Girlfriend . . . well, she gave me most of hers, but I'm sure that's because she loves me.

That's Not Really Cooking

When it comes to my culinary exploits, The Girlfriend, to her credit, has been willing to try every crazy idea I've suggested, even the ones that came with disclaimers:

"I *think* this should taste alright . . . if not I can add some parsley or something."

"The recipe calls for three eggs and we only had one, so I tried to adjust the amount of everything else."

"Okay, I know the crust came out more *spongy* than flaky, but hey, the filling has chocolate in it!"

She has also indulged me by being putting up with a lot more of the Food Network than anyone should have to endure. "They're doing another season of 'Food Truck Wars, honey!"

It would be different if I were *using* what I learn on these shows in making dinner for us, but I can't remember the last time I had to chiffonade some kale.

I really should stop watching cooking shows on television altogether. First of all, if she knows I'm watching them, they set up unrealistic expectations on the home front.

Also, it's frustrating for me, because I'll get inspired by something I see, and then I look in our pantry and fridge and realize I don't have a lot of the ingredients they use on those shows..

Since she knows what I've been watching, we'll have conversations like,

"What did you learn to cook today?"
"Oh, they made a lobster bisque with black truffle shavings. But . . . *we're* having elbow macaroni with ground beef. Enjoy!"

It must make you a little crazy to host a cooking show, because there isn't usually an audience, and without one, you're pretty much talking to yourself for half an hour. Which I would be doing anyway, so I'm a natural!

I thought I'd stumbled on a whole new genre of cooking show when I was in the other room and overheard the host say "Let's take a look at my breasts, now."

Unfortunately she was checking on some chicken, not cooking topless, but that would be a great show. I can imagine the warning: "Mature audiences. Adult content. Mild splattering."

I also did a double take when I heard "It's time for each chef to 'grab his wahoo,' but apparently that's a type of fish.

Cooking shows never seem realistic to me, because nothing ever goes wrong. Horribly wrong, like when I'm trying to make a beautiful casserole in carefully constructed layers and then decide "Screw it, I'll just mix it all up and bake the hell out of it for an hour."

Sometimes when I'm putting a dish together I'll just grab a couple of random spices I haven't tried and throw 'em in, which I suppose could be risky . . .

What if oregano and say, turmeric, when combined over heat, actually cause some sort of explosive reaction that takes out the whole kitchen. I just don't know.

Cooking for two has been an adjustment, because now my 'experiments' are her dinner-after-a-long-work-day. Cooking for someone else has also helped me understand why moms for centuries have yelled, "Get out of my kitchen while I'm cooking."

It isn't that I don't enjoy some company while I'm working. But for one thing, my kitchen is never as organized as the ones on tv.

On top of that, *I'm* not organized, so sometimes I end up running around like a lunatic, frantically flinging things I've forgotten into pots and pans until our kitchen looks like a Jackson Pollock painting.

And sometimes I *might* accidentally drop something on the floor that needs to go in the dish, and I *might* pick it up and put it back in the skillet. The heat will kill any germs, right? Nobody needs to know that happened.

The Food Network hosts also never swear, which really makes me question their credibility. Showtime should launch a cooking show in which the chefs are allowed to say the things *real* cooks say at home.

"Where the f*** is my rolling pin?" "What the ****? This is moldy already?" "****, that's way too much ************* rosemary!"

Despite the swearing and occasional pain I've endured when trying the cooking thing, there's a part of me that enjoys it more than writing.

It's one thing to create something that, *if* it gets published, *might* become popular. But if I *cook* something and it *works*, it feels real on a whole other level.

I'm not deluded enough to think my writing will have any lasting impact. But The Girlfriend *still* remembers the Garlic and Mustard Brushed Chicken Breast Stuffed with Spinach that I made *two months ago.*

The Girlfriend Draws the Line

Since I do all the cooking, I usually put together the grocery list, and so far, we've only had a few shopping gaffes.

I think I've finally gotten her to stop buying things we don't need *simply* because they're on sale *("Yes, dear, that is a good price for bok choy . . . but neither of us eat bok choy.")*

Likewise, I think she gets that, for a multitude of reasons, if you *must* buy a chemical-laden industrially-processed fake whipped topping, you get the Redi-Whip, not the Cool-Whip, if only because you can squirt it directly into your mouth, bypassing the need to make dessert at all.

I've learned over time that, despite my loving partner's willingness to play along with my faux-foodie aspirations, there are things she would rather not eat.

Capers received a distinctly tepid response; collard greens were NOT the hit I had expected; she's not into cucumbers, and despite my belief that broccoli and cauliflower make a perfect veggie combo, the cauliflower part leaves her cold.

At first I thought she had some rare psychological trauma involving foods that start with the letter 'c.' But it turns out, she's fine with couscous, and that has *two* 'c's.

Bottom line, relationships are about compromise, so I've resigned myself to the fact that she'll never experience my fabulous caper-cucumber crusted cauliflower, with a side of collard greens.

We don't have a lot of extra cash, so I don't lobby for a lot of cooking gadgets. Besides, with my long history of clumsiness, some gadgets are out of the question.

I don't imagine she'll ever buy me an electric knife, for example, since that would simply allow me to cut myself more quickly and efficiently.

But there is one food-related device that I have wanted since the first time I saw it. This is a thingamajig so cool, on so many levels, that *I* would instantly become cooler *simply by owning one.*

You probably already know what I'm building to here. It's a jerky gun.

Some quotes from the catalog:

"The one and only Jerky Gun" (*as opposed to all those knockoff jerky weapons you see on the street?*).

"This item is made to give years of performance" ("*Kids, this was your great grandpa's jerky gun…*").

Load the barrel of the Jerky Gun with lean, seasoned ground meat and shoot out flat strips of jerky or round snack sticks (*Because it's my Second Amendment right to bear arms...that shoot meat snacks*).

In addition, the barrel will hold three-quarters of a pound of meat, though I've heard stories of street gangs that illegally modify these to hold a full pound.

Incidentally, the gun in the picture comes with three nozzles and enough seasoning for 4 pounds of meat. Complete instructions included, but I'm sure most of us were taught from an early age how to responsibly shoot meat products out of a gun.

Now this same company also sells a Jerky Cannon and, for you fans of overkill, a Jerky Cannon DOUBLE BARREL! Now THAT would obviously be ridiculous–the Jerky Gun is all we need.

Fifty bucks. Yeah, that's a hard one to pitch: "Hey hon, how was your day? Cool. Listen, I went ahead and put fifty bucks on the card for that jerky gun I was telling you about . . . ?"

I'm not sure exactly what her objection was, but she drew the line. Maybe it was just the 'gun' part of the concept–and maybe she was worried that if we had one in the house, according to statistics, someone could break in and use our jerky gun against us.

Or it could have been the jerky part. In my excitement over FINDING jerky weaponry, I had forgotten that I actually don't *like* jerky. The idea just seems wrong.

Eating jerky is like saying, "I enjoy the *flavor* of meat, but I'd like it to be all dried out, and harder to chew." Or maybe if you need food that you can . . . mail in an envelope.

I didn't push very hard for the meat musket. You pick your battles when you're part of a couple. And we've learned to negotiate–we respected each other's opinions, and reached a compromise. I agreed to not buy the Jerky Gun, and she agreed to not let me.

It wasn't anything like that whole ugly Redi-Whip fiasco. Anyway, I figure if I give up on the gun, she'll give in on the nifty zester I *really* need.

I Baked A Pie!

Until recently, I had an irrational fear of something most cooks take in stride . . . baking. And for anyone who thought the answer should have been 'blowing up the kitchen in yet another experiment,' that's not an *irrational* fear.

I'm not afraid of baked *goods*, mind you–there are very few things I *wouldn't* eat if they came stuffed inside a pastry. I *have* been afraid of actually *baking*, though.

The shows on the food channels don't help, because the projects you see on a show like 'Cupcake Wars' are a bit over the top for the aspiring home baker:

> "For this challenge, we want you to make a cupcake version of the Louvre and recreate all of its paintings with only frosting and chocolate jimmies–you have fifteen minutes."

It's been said that baking is a science, whereas cooking is an art. Don't get me wrong -- science has its place. My problem is, art leaves room for mistakes, and science, not so much.

In art, you can make mistakes that end up looking brilliant, as long as people know it was supposed to be art.

Maybe early in his career, Picasso just couldn't draw very well, but people thought he intentionally drew misshapen faces *("You wanna call it 'cubism,' fine, but that's SO not what I was going for.")*

On the other hand, if you make a mistake with a pie or a cake, you can't just tweak it as you go along, and I'm used to some margin for error.

So I acknowledge that I'm afraid making dessert. Your cakes, your pies. The kind of baking that seems to require either

- learning recipes from Grandma that have been passed down for generations OR
- paying attention to details in following directions exactly as written while using advanced calculus

Now as for the first approach, though my mom baked cookies every Christmas, and I suppose I 'helped,' all I remember is thinking "I can't believe I have to crack all these walnuts. I don't even like walnuts."

And as for the other method, let's just say I've never checked the box marked 'attention to detail' when I've listed my strengths on a job application. But I have had enough therapy to know that you should always face your fears, so I decided to bake a pie . . .

I remembered that dough was made from flour, and I had some flour. Also, I was pretty sure that butter was involved.

I found a recipe for a "Quick and Easy Pie Crust." It called for flour and butter (and some process called 'folding the butter in," which seemed to me overly fussy so I opted to just put the butter in the bowl and mix it all by hand.)

This, in retrospect, was a mistake, and probably accounts for the reference in the recipe to using "two forks or a pastry cutter."

About a half hour later, I had removed most of the gooey proto-dough from my hands and had something in the bowl I could work with.

At this point I noticed that pie crust recipes seem to always include something called 'baking soda,' which I didn't have. Oh, well.

For the filling, I turned once again to my little one-button chopper. I threw in a bunch of peanut butter.

After initially trying to melt some Hershey's Kisses in a ramekin that turned out to not be ENTIRELY microwave-safe, I finished melting the chocolate in a saucepan.

Then I added the chocolate to the peanut butter, along with some vanilla extract and a banana.

Lastly, I pushed the 'pulse' button several times, stopping occasionally to shove the banana to the bottom (I realize that 'shove' isn't a word you find in a lot of cookbooks.)

I tasted it, and determined it was pie-worthy. I also determined that if the crust didn't come out right, I had made a really good pudding.

I put the dough in my pie dish and spread it more or less evenly. Then I spent ten minutes repairing holes in the crust, a laborious process in which I grab some dough to 'patch' the holes.

After chilling the crust for a few minutes, I added the filling and put it in the oven. I had to figure out how long it should bake, but I couldn't find anything online for "Peanut Butter Chocolate Banana Pie in a Crust Made Without Baking Powder."

So I *averaged* how long various pies called for and decided on fifteen minutes at 425 followed by forty-five minutes at 350. Already, baking was feeling like way too much math.

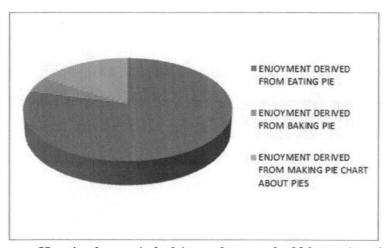

Here's the weird thing–about a half hour in, the apartment started to smell like . . . pie! *Homemade* pie! I'll be honest–the crust was a little overdone. It was also whatever the opposite of 'flaky' would be.

I felt a little pressure to make this work. I had used the last of The Girlfriend's chocolate to make the filling while she was at work, and you need to be pretty damned sure of yourself if you're willing to risk the last of a woman's chocolate.

But when it was time for dessert, she and I agreed that, for the most part, it was like eating actual pie. I'm sure the artificially-flavored, artificially-colored, partially hydrogenated Cool Whip helped, but underneath *that* was a real homemade pie.

> *Update: Since this attempt, I have tried to make a pie crust twice, and both times they were slightly off. Then I figured out what I had been doing wrong: I wasn't buying pre-made pie crusts.*

The World According to Stan

I'm sure this next statement will cause me to lose any respect I may have gained from actual foodies along the way, but here goes: 'gourmet comfort food' is a stupid concept.

I've learned to appreciate the nuances of fine dining, but part of what I love about what's called comfort food is the fact that it's NOT a culinary adventure—I want it to *comfort* me, not make me wonder what it is.

I want it to evoke memories, not provoke discussions. For me, 'gourmet comfort food' is like 'Congressional efficiency,' or 'rowdy James Taylor fans.'

Let's look at the doughnut (if you have a doughnut handy, go ahead, and grab it while you read the rest of this). First off, it's round. There's the circle of life, right there.

Some doughnuts have holes in the middle, just like some people's lives. Some are filled with sweetness, again, just like some lives.

Not that I'm much of a flag-waver, but the doughnut is also Americana to me. Sure, Europe has its pastries, and some of them are even deep-fried.

I'd hate to get angry letters from Dutch people because I neglected their *olykoeken*, but c'mon—it literally means 'oily cakes.'

And yes, I know that the French word 'beignet' essentially means 'fried dough,' and that the Italian 'zeppole' is from an Arabic word for 'fried dough,' but these cultures have other food traditions which made them famous.

But the first reference to the word 'doughnut' is in an essay by the American, Washington Irving, so there. America was *built* on fried dough.

When I see a doughnut shop, I don't want to see the words 'reinvent,' 'conceptualize, or 'deconstruct.' Likewise, the phrase 'flavor profile.' I want to see words like 'hot,' 'fresh,' and 'filled.' Maybe the phrase 'free refills.'

The most profound food memory I have is of a doughnut shop (one 'p,' no 'e') in a part of L.A. called Westwood, a couple blocks from my *almost mater*, U.C.L.A.

Stan's Doughnuts opened in 1965, and between 1978 and 1982, I must have eaten several hundred of Stan's signature Peanut Butter Pockets. Sometimes I'd go crazy and have the Peanut Butter Pocket *with Banana* (these were my wild college years, after all).

When I decided to write about Stan's, I wanted people to see what the joint looks like, so I called the number I found online, to ask for permission to use a couple of the pictures I found online. At this point, I didn't even know if there was a real Stan.

I wanted there to be a Stan. There is something comforting (that word again!) about a business whose name consists entirely of the owner's name and what he sells. There's accountability.

"Who's responsible for these doughnuts?" "Oh, that's Stan. I'll get him for you." If I could find this mythical "Stan,' I would know that a real person stood behind a real product, and you don't see that often these days.

I would always rather take my car to Jim's Auto Repair than someplace called 'Autopia,' and I'd trust the calamari at a place called Giuseppi's Seafood over, say, some place called the Shrimp Shack. If you're willing to put your name on the sign, I'm willing to do business with you.

So I was delighted to discover that there is, in fact, a real Stan. Not only is Stan *real*, he's at the shop when I call.

After a perfunctory introduction (*"I'm a humor writer and I'd like to talk with you for something I'm writing"*), he tells me I can use the pictures. "A hundred percent—no problem!" Then he added one of those phrases you can only get away with if you've really lived, saying "It's a round world."

He seemed *so* accommodating, I decided to push my luck, and I asked him if I could call him back with a few questions. I didn't take any journalism classes in college, but I had a feeling this guy might have a few stories to tell, so we set up a phone interview.

I called on the day before he turned eighty-two, as it turned out, but as soon as we started recording, I knew he had at least ten times as many stories as he'd had birthdays.

You need to know that Stan opened "Stan's" in a part of L.A that was known for college students and movie glitz (studios have for years premiered important films at the theaters in Westwood Village).

It was also a time when psychedelia was just starting to seep into pop culture, and pop culture was getting a lot less 'white bread'—1965 gave us hits by the Mindbenders and the Strangeloves, but it also gave us James Brown.

There was a lot of heady stuff going on, and a man less sure of his vision might have given in to the temptation to be trendy, but not Stan Berman. He opened a doughnut shop.

I asked him how he got started in the doughnut biz, and he told the story of approaching the owner of a well-known grocery store in L.A. (Gelson's) about putting his doughnuts in there. Gelson's, of course, now has a bakery, but they don't have a Stan's–

> "We approached Bernie Gelson, and (he) said he couldn't give us three parking spaces to build the doughnut shop, because those three parking spaces would produce so much income. . . "

He was born in 1929 in Philadelphia; his father and grandfather both were bakers, but Stan also studied accounting. He was drafted into the Marine Corps in '51, and

> "Believe it or not. . . I wound up being a baker in the Marine Corps, which never really happened– usually a baker became a machine-gunner, or whatever else...

I wanted to know the strangest request he'd ever gotten from a regular customer, and here's where Stan was way ahead of the curve...

> "Now this was forty-some years ago, this happened. Somebody came in, and said they loved peanut butter, and (asked) if I could make a doughnut with peanut butter.
>
> And so I said, "I never heard of such a thing." So she went to the market and bought me a jar of peanut butter.
>
> And we played around with it, first, like a jelly doughnut *(which he explained meant frying it, THEN filling it)*, and it just didn't have it. So I decided to try and seal that . . . to make a pocket, put the peanut butter in, and <u>then</u> fry it."

This 'weird' idea became Stan's most famous creation, which he has for years called a Reese's Peanut Butter Pocket.

Here was my chance to earn my reporter's stripes–my Woodward-Bernstein moment. Playing it a coyly, I said I was "a little confused about the Reese's thing–you're not connected to the company that *makes* Reese's, are you?

"No, are you kidding? That's the reason I <u>did</u> that! I was hoping some day they would come here, and tell me they're suing me, and that I should stop using their name–and they never did!"

Stan also revealed that, for a while, he called his creation *Al's* Peanut Butter Pocket. Apparently this 'Al' would park his limo in front of the place, sit at the counter, eat half a dozen, and take half a dozen to go.

A few days later, Al was back and placed the same order…

"He was a New York character, and through this doughnut we became friends. Eventually I found out who it was, and after about a year, I decided to change the name to 'Al's.'"

"The guy's name was Al Goldstein. He had his headquarters in New York, but he came here to see all the porno people."

Not surprisingly, I didn't have a follow-up question ready.

I hadn't expected to learn that Stan was friends with the publisher of 'Screw' magazine. Then I got it! Fried dough has the power to bring people together! Preppie or a pornographer, Stan didn't judge.

'The Reese's thing' wasn't Stan's only brush with trademark issues. The building he took over in '65 had been an 'Orange Julius,' but though he had the five grand for the building, he didn't have the twenty-five grand to renew the franchise.

Undaunted (and I can't imagine Stan *ever* being 'daunted'), he simply changed it to an 'Orange *Jubilee.'*

"I had a food chemist friend, and we took the Orange Julius powder, and we reproduced it. We put a hat on the little figurine they use, and we dressed him up a little, and I think instead of a sword, we made it, like, a broom, or whatever. . .

We're getting ready to open, that day, and these two giants walk through my doors, they just can fit and they're like seven-foot doors. . .

They're wearing beautiful suits, dressed to kill, and they say, "You're infringing on Orange Julius, and we're here to tell you to close. Period."

Naturally, *Stan's* came through it fine. Apparently his neighbor two doors down was a lawyer who happened to be president of the company which happened to own Orange Julius. The two 'giants' came back the next day and said that Stan could stay open. Now that's American ingenuity!

Who knew there was this much intrigue and subterfuge in the pastry industry?

We know about Stan's business acumen. I wanted to know if he ever had an idea for a type doughnut that flopped. He thought for only a second or two and then declared,

> "Yeah. I tried something with kiwi. I tried kiwi. It never worked. Never, never worked."

Shifting gears (in case the kiwi incident was still a touchy subject), I asked him what it was like in the late sixties, with his shop adjacent to a major university as protests were beginning to explode.

His answer had a special kind of wisdom to it, and, I believe, a twinge of sadness:

> "It was amazing. The turmoil was here, and except for a few happenings, most of it was really before the advent of the gun. Everything happened when these kids discovered the gun, in the eighties.
>
> But in the sixties, seventies—they didn't know about a gun. And so, whenever there was a problem, there was a fistfight, somebody got hit with a stick. . . but no guns. You didn't hear of a shooting at a riot."

Being in an area with several first-run movie theaters, Stan has seen plenty of celebs, and the great thing is he doesn't come across overly star-struck, but he's not jaded either. In fact, he told me a sweet story about Gilda Radner...

> "She was a junk-food eater . . . you don't know this . . . she would come in with her husband, a guy named Gene Wilder.
>
> They came in about five or ten days before she passed, and I would give her a doughnut, and Gene would just . . . sit against the wall, drink a cup of coffee, and watch her."

Early in the interview, I asked him if he was happy he didn't become an accountant. He said, "Life has been a bowl of cherries, kiddo," and I bought every word. Even 'kiddo.' Because I think Stan is the real deal.

Stan was right. It is a round world, but if you do it right, it can be filled with peanut butter and fresh banana, and topped with banana frosting and chocolate chips.

So there's a little deep fried wisdom. But the most important thing I learned from Stan? Kiwi doughnuts are a bad idea.

In Which I Pester a Real Chef

I suppose I'm a food writer now, since this is a book about food, but it's not the sort of writing I imagined doing for my first book.

I fancied myself being a novelist one day, but I have to admit I'm just not that *organized*. I don't remember things I wrote last week, so it seemed a bit out of my reach to keep track of multiple characters over hundreds of pages AND have the story make sense.

> *"His first novel was marred by the recurrence of the main character years after being killed, and by several chapters that seemed to be from an entirely different novel."*

I also fancied myself a screenwriter for a time, until I realized that every possible story idea has already been made into a movie. Of course, if they ever find a way to have cowboys and aliens fight some *pirates*, it would be the coolest movie ever.

When I was still doing standup, I went through a very brief and regrettable phase where I called myself a 'comedy journalist.' Although I understand now how insufferably pretentious that was, I still love the IDEA of being a reporter.

From "The Front Page" to "All The President's Men" (I even watched "Lou Grant"). I've always been drawn to the hard-boiled, cynical journalist, press pass shoved in the brim of his hat, tilting against the windmills of corruption.

TELL ME THE REAL STORY BEHIND THIS MEATLOAF OF YOURS...

I have found a way to channel my inner Murrow with occasional interviews of people on the fringes of the food scene.

Emboldened by my hard-hitting look at an L.A. doughnut shop, I decided to interview an actual chef, silly hat and all. Looking back, I probably didn't need to wear the hat.

Before talking to a real, working chef, I faced two distinct, but equally daunting challenges.

- I didn't know what to ask a real, working chef.
- I didn't know any real, working chefs.

For the questions, I just wanted to avoid clichés and ask things he doesn't usually get asked, just to get some insight into the culinary mind.

For my subject, I figured it would make sense to start with someone local, and thankfully, a dear friend was able to introduce me to Bret Bannon.

Bret isn't just a top-notch chef, mind you; he teaches private classes, he's on the faculty at a well-respected cooking school, he apprenticed under noted chocolatier B.T. McElrath, and he leads popular culinary tours of France.

Beyond those accomplishments, he's got a great name. 'Bret Bannon' sounds like a private-eye in a morally ambiguous film noir, as in, *"NOBODY double-crosses Bret Bannon!"*

Or maybe 'Bret Bannon' is the 'by day' identity of a superhero: *"By day, he's mild-mannered culinary instructor Bret Bannon–by night, he's known as . . .*

Despite saying at one point *"I don't have a funny bone in my body"* (something I might have wanted to know before I asked him a bunch of oddball questions), he was charming and handled the interview with aplomb.

I started by asking him what kind of music he listens to when he's cooking:

> "I generally don't listen to music when I'm cooking. If there are people over, I would rather have conversation, and not have to try to talk over music."

Okay. Maybe music wasn't the ice-breaker I thought it would be.

When I asked him to remember the first meal he ever prepared for someone important, he couldn't remember the meal but remembered this:

"Mother's Day breakfast for my mom. I made coffee, and it looked a little weak, so I added instant coffee. It was awful."

I think it's comforting for the average cook at home to realize that everyone who cooks makes mistakes, so I asked him to tell me about his worst kitchen disaster:

"I tried a new recipe, and cooked the caramel too long. It was like cement."

For some perspective, I've caused a blender to explode, covering my kitchen in liquefied corn, and I've dropped an entire meatloaf minutes before serving. But I still feel we bonded on that one.

Then I suggested a scenario from a chef's nightmare: If, for the rest of your life, you could only use one spice in your cooking (not counting salt and pepper), what would it be?" After considerable thought, he chose 'garam masala.'

I didn't learn until after the interview that garam masala is actually a *blend* of spices.

The Punjabi version of garam masala typically includes black and white peppercorns, cloves, malabar leaves, mace blades, black and white cumin seeds . . . also cinnamon, black, brown and green cardamom pods, nutmeg, star anise and coriander seeds.

I'm sure Bret *knew* that garam masala wasn't just *one* spice. He was just dodging my line of questioning. Very crafty, Mr. Bannon. Very crafty indeed.

Now it was time to get hypothetical: If you had a time machine, where, and during what historical era, would you like to be a cook? Turns out, he loves France (how unusual for a chef, right?), but he added

> "I don't know if I'd want to be a cook during Louie XIV's era... I'd rather be a participant."

One more 'what if': A wealthy benefactor wants you to cook one dish that best represents your style and your strengths. What do you cook? After a long pause, he said,

> "Probably . . . a cassoulet."

I started thinking about this marvelous, hearty Provencal stew when–I had it!

That's our superhero's name -- *Captain Cassoulet*!!! Now I just have to design a cape, and a toque with special powers!

I could tell my relentless questioning was making Chef Bannon sweat, but he tried to play along . . . until a simple question about hotdish caused his story to unravel.

To give things a local spin, I asked him how he might put a gourmet spin on the beloved Minnesota classic known as Tater Tot Hotdish.

> "I'd probably make my own tater tots. If I remember correctly, you grate the potatoes, and then you add a little bit of gelatin, then you hydrate it.
> Then you roll it with any other spices into a cylinder that's about an inch in diameter; then you refrigerate it, and you cut it, and you deep fry them."

Something didn't seem quite right. Maybe it was the word 'gelatin' that put me off. Sure, he could *describe* tater tots, but did he really *understand* what they represent in the broader context of the hotdish? Then, the bombshell:

> "I've actually never made tater tot hotdish."

Finally, after minutes of exhaustive research and tireless digging (okay, I was a little tired), I had uncovered some dirt! I could sell this to '*TMZ*!'

MINNESOTA CHEF CONFESSES: ## "I'VE NEVER MADE TATER TOT HOTDISH!"

As Seen On TV

I'm not usually tempted by infomercials, other than the Time-Life Ultimate Rock Ballads collection. You can't blame me there—it had that one Glass Tiger song . . . how is that NOT worth $118?

But give me a half-hour pitch for some new kitchen gadget, and I will stare at the tv transfixed, wondering, "How have I managed to even *feed myself* without one of these?"

The Girlfriend wasn't on board with us getting a Jerky Gun™, since we *technically* didn't need one, so now I try to appeal to reason. And if television has taught me anything, it's that my way of doing things in the kitchen will just lead to spills, messes, and wasted money.

Why, according to an ad I saw for some vacuumy-sealer thing, last year alone I threw away more than *five hundred thousand dollars in food!*

I wasn't into cooking when Ginsu Knives came out, and since I've started taking cooking seriously, I've still never needed to slice through an aluminum can.

I *have* considered plunking down the hundred bucks for a Magic Bullet set, partly because it's the only infomercial product I know of named after an assassination conspiracy theory. Besides, what if it's really magical?

That's how they suck me in. I know most of the products advertised on late night television are crap, but what if *this one* really *is* 'revolutionary?'

In that case I'd be an idiot *not* to buy it, especially if they're throwing in a second one 'absolutely free!'

Consider the Magic Bullet. First, it has a high-torque power base, and I think it was the great chef Escoffier who said, *"La cuisine est tout au sujet du couple, bébé!"* That's right; I looked up the French word for 'torque.'

Naturally, you get your cross blade and your flat blade, your tall AND short bullet cups, some steamer/shaker tops, and your resealable containers. You also get party mugs with 'comfort lip rings,' because who **hasn't** had a party ruined by uncomfortable mugs?

At this point I'm sure you're thinking "That's probably all there is," but in fact...THERE'S MORE! There's a Magic Bullet Cookbook that's worth the hundred bucks by itself–if only because it includes a recipe for 'snazzy egg salad.' I've made egg salad before, but it's *never* had any snazz!

And they'll throw in a blender, *and* a juicer that "works as easily as the two-hundred dollar juicers." You know, those two-hundred dollar juicers so many of us grew up with. That's twenty-one pieces of time-saving convenience!

Which isn't as impressive as the Cake Pops kit. That has *twenty-five* pieces, although, to be fair, eighteen of those are the sticks you use to hold the cake pops. I'm just sayin', the sticks should only count as one item.

Weirdest part of the Cake Pops ad is when they talk about not wanting to deal with "the hassle of cake." Because after dealing with "The Man," cake *is* probably the biggest source of hassle in my life.

I own one "As Seen On TV" product. As a birthday gift, a friend bought me a Slap-Chop. I love how prosaic that name is. No exaggerated, mystical claims here . . . you slap it, it chops things.

This is great for people who feel the normal chopping experience isn't violent enough, and I have to say, you can release a surprising amount of aggression with just a little bit of slap-chopping.

Just make sure, if you want one, that you act now, because I think they said supplies are limited.

Around the same time of night when you might see a Slap-Chop ad, there are also a huge number of career oriented ads, but I don't imagine they're very effective. I'm pretty sure most people watching basic cable at four in the morning have already made peace with *not* having a job.

No matter which barely-accredited essentially-fictional school is being pitched, the ads are the same.It's always perky people telling their friends about the rewards of an exciting career at the cutting edge of tomorrow's jobs in the growing field of computer science. Or refrigeration and heating.

I saw the same woman on two *different* ads. Apparently she's taking a double major in dental hygiene *and* motorcycle repair. Good for her.

What really caught my attention was an ad for Le Cordon Bleu, because they have an *online* program! Really? How does that work? Unless Apple has come up with a computer interface that allows you to taste or smell what you cooked, how would they know if you passed?

I wouldn't use the word 'regret,' but I will say that I *wish* I had discovered my inner foodie when I was younger, because I would have thought about culinary school. I've always envied people whose educational choice might lead to an actual job.

My last major of record was English, so clearly by that point I'd given up on the idea of 'earning a living.' I constantly had to answer the question, "What are you gonna DO with your degree?"

If I'd been in *cooking* school, it would have been so much easier. I could have said "I'm gonna *cook*, dumbass."

The Culinary Institute of America is, I suppose, the Harvard of cooking schools, and their curriculum features all the classes you might expect in food preparation, food safety, nutrition . . .

The school also offers something called 'meat fabrication,' which sounds a little too Orwellian for my tastes *("Workers will be given their lunches once the meat is fabricated").*

I might have seriously considered a career at the cutting edge of tomorrow's jobs in the growing field of meat fabrication, until I found out how much a culinary education costs. At the Institute, tuition is just over fifty thousand dollars.

Now I know why duck confit is so expensive. Hell, the duck probably only costs ten bucks . . . the other thirty goes to paying off the chef's student loans!

At this stage of my life, though, if I somehow came across fifty grand, I think I'd pass on culinary school. Instead, I'd invest that money in some sort of cooking gadget that I could sell in a half-hour show.

All you have to do is tell people that the way they've always done some kitchen task is "too much hassle" or "throwing money down the drain." Maybe add the phrase "space-age technology."

Sure, I'd have to spend money on a B-grade celebrity spokesperson ("Now here's TV's Scott Baio with a testimonial for the revolutionary new Asparagus Master!"). I'd also need to invent something, but after that, it's pure profit.

Maybe I'll create a quinoa sifter ("Tired of sifting your quinoa the old-fashioned way?"), or specially-designed broccoli tongs.

I have an idea for a kitchen device that is just begging to be invented, but since I have no mechanical aptitude and can't draw, I have decided to give away my idea. All I ask is, if you *do* something with it, let me do the ad

Here's the kitchen necessity that everybody's talking about –The Flipper!

> "Are you spending *too much time* flipping your omelets by hand? Do you always *overcook* one side of the pancake? Tired of burgers sticking to supposedly *non-stick* pans *because you didn't flip them in time*? How many meals have you *ruined* with flimsy spatulas?
>
> *Stop* ruining your family's meals -- you need The Flipper! Powered by the same technology used in NASA's advanced weather satellites, a tiny patented mechanism activates the Turbo Food Paddles on The Flipper, so you can serve perfectly-flipped food every time!
>
> But that's not all! If you call in the next twenty seconds, we'll throw in the Kitchen Sorcery Wand for free, and we're not even sure what it does!
>
> In fact, we'll give you *ten* of them for free, along with a stylish faux-naugahyde carrying case!"

Knowing What's Good for You

As the de facto menu planner for our non-traditional quasi-family unit, I try to make sure The Girlfriend and I eat a healthy, balanced diet. Granted, our definition of 'balanced' might be different than yours.

For instance, we believe that, if you had a salad for dinner, you can, and probably should, have a gigantic apple fritter for dessert. You know, for *balance*.

In general, we eat healthy food, and we both had to relearn some things. For instance, I had to explain that neither ice cream nor chocolate is, *per se*, a 'food group.'

But what does healthy mean, exactly? Now, I'm sure even ravenous meat-eaters would probably agree vegetables are involved, in some way.

Growing up, I never had a problem eating my vegetables, because if they were on my dinner plate, I was supposed to eat them.

Of course, Mom never exactly challenged our palates — the Great Kale Experiment of the early seventies notwithstanding.

I was a vegetarian for two weeks in 1987, a commitment which, in retrospect, lasted longer than a lot of my relationships in 1987.

I might have stayed with it, too, except that in the eighties, I was on the road all the time, and options for the aspiring herbivore were limited at your various Perkins and Stuckey's locations. You get really tired of iceberg lettuce and warm ranch dressing.

I don't imagine there were too many vegetarian dining options in the seventeenth century, but in 1622, the first 'health food' cookbook was published by Tobias Venner called

> *"Via Recta ad Vitam Longam, or a Plaine Philosophical Discourse of the Nature, Faculties, and Effects of all suche things as by way of Nourishments and Dietetical Observations made for the Preservation of Health."*

The catchy title translates as either 'The Straight Road to Long Life' or 'Avoid Eating at the Olive Garden' (my Latin is sketchy at best). His advice:

> "Cut down on heavy sauces, meats and desserts" and "Avoid eating at Ye Olde Olive Garden, despite the unlimited breadsticks, for that will surely lead to ill humours,

Ellen Swallow Richards is credited with the first American health food cookbook, called *"First Lessons in Food and Diet,"* in 1904.

At the time, she was already known for the success of her earlier books. At the turn of the twentieth century, the hipsters were all reading her classic, *"The Effect of Heat on the Digestibility of Gluten."*

Fans of ESW raved about her provocative book, *"The Adulterations of Groceries,"* which also might be the title of a Merchant-Ivory film.

I did some research on Ms. Richards, and I'm not trying to turn my little column into a post-feminist screed here, but I have a question . . .

WHY IS THIS WOMAN NOT FAMOUS?

Ellen Swallow Richards (1842-1911)

**FIRST AMERICAN WOMAN ADMITTED TO A SCHOOL OF SCIENCE
FIRST AMERICAN WOMAN TO EARN A DEGREE IN CHEMISTRY.
FIRST WOMAN ADMITTED TO M.I.T.
FIRST FEMALE INSTRUCTOR AT M.I.T.**

One would think that the history books could give us one less paragraph on, for instance, the Monroe Doctrine to make a little room for Ms. Richards.

About a century after Ellen Swallow Richards, the USDA introduced the first 'food pyramid,' but it was doomed to failure. C'mon, people . . . Americans don't remember their high school geometry! For the average American, you might as well have called it a Food Dodecahedron.

Recently, the USDA replaced the Food Pyramid with the even more remedial 'Choose My Plate.' But there will still be confused people wondering, "Do I *have* to have dairy with grains" and "Is this part of the socialist takeover of the government Fox News mentioned?"

Other countries have tried to get creative with the whole "If we draw a *picture* of what they should eat maybe they won't get fat like Americans" thing.

In France they have twenty-five *separate* nutrition guides, NONE of which are followed by the French. And Canada has a Food Rainbow. Of course they do.

The Chinese use a Food Pagoda, whereas in Japan, it's a spinning top. Too bad the Japanese couldn't find a way to use anime, because a hot alien chick with a machine gun could get a lot of teenage boys on the right nutritional path.

Forget foods you *should* eat — I'm just glad there aren't many foods I *can't* eat. I don't eat much dairy, but I don't like to say I'm lactose intolerant, because, frankly, I'm a liberal, and I feel I should stand up to intolerance. So if I have a little cheese once in a while, I'm making a political statement.

The intersection of politics and food has given us the 'locavore,' which, if I understand it correctly, means I can only eat Chilean sea bass at *local* restaurants.

If there are 'locavores,' why not '*loco*vores,' who only buy their food from crazy people? Or maybe we could call people who only eat bland, boring foods 'borivores.' And of course, if you keep strictly kosher, you're a Torahvore! I got a million of 'em!

Of course, in addition to vegetarians, there are vegans and then there are '*fruit*arians,' who I can only imagine are even **more** judgmental than vegans.

And if the only animals you eat are seafood, I believe that makes you a 'pesceterian,' although maybe the 'Pescetarians' are a religious cult devoted to annoying people.

I have trouble keeping track of what I'm supposed to eat. There's always some new healthy grain or super fruit or must-have amino acid. At this point, I figure I'm as qualified as anyone to toss out random diet suggestions. So if the following diets work for you, great!

THE LEXICOGRAVORE DIET

First, assign a letter, in order, to each day of the month. You only are allowed on a given date to eat foods that start with that date's letter. So, on the first of the month, you can eat apricots, artichokes, avocado . . . for day two you've got your bacon, maybe some blueberries, even brisket!

After day twenty-six, you can eat what you want until the first of the month, when it's back to arugula, or maybe alligator. Also, on day twenty-four, you can eat what you want because no foods start with 'x.'

THE CARTOGRAVORE DIET

Get out your placemat with the big map of the U.S. on it, because, on this diet, you will only be able to eat official state foods, and you'll be eating them in the order the states were admitted to the Union!

On day one, how about carving up Delaware's state bird and enjoying some blue hen? Sure, it's their state *bird*, not their state food, but if you cook it right . . . Day two is cheesesteak, and you might want to fill up on it, because for New Jersey's day, all you get is a tomato.

The rest of your first week includes Georgia grits (technically their official state 'prepared dish'), but plan ahead, because Connecticut has no state food, so on day five, you don't eat at all. Just be careful on day seventeen, because too much Ohio pawpaw probably isn't good for anybody.

The creepily named 'Center for Science in the Public Interest' recently put together a list of the ten healthiest foods.

Sadly, none of them are pastries. However, fans of butternut squash (you know who you are) should feel vindicated.

Every few years we find out something is bad for you that we thought was just fine. It was easier to be healthy when I was younger, because we didn't know as much!

"Why, when I was your age we only had ONE kind of cholesterol, and we weren't sure whether it was good or bad for you!"

Let's be honest. We all have a vague idea of what 'healthy' is, but we crave the crap. And to me, that's part of a balanced diet, too.

But if I'm gonna eat something I KNOW is bad for me, I don't need to find out HOW bad.

I've never understood why, for example, Hostess would bother to list 'nutritional information' for their 'fruit' pies.

I guess it's useful to know that if you eat one, you'll get two percent of the calcium and four percent of the phosphorus you should be getting in your daily diet.

By my math, that means that if you eat twenty-five pies a day, you'll get all the phosphorus you need!

What I love about this wrapper is that it's a "real fruit pie" (there's even a picture of real fruit to prove it), yet, if you look closely, the food wizards at Hostess realized it still needed to be "artificially flavored."I picture one of the product guys at a meeting saying,

> "Yeah, I'm on board with the real fruit, but here's another direction we could go: we take the fruit and whatever boring 'real' flavor it has and then we add more flavor *artificially*!

By contrast, the label on this organic pasta may be the ultimate example of truth in labeling. Much more than the nit-picky specifics of *what* the ingredients are, I just want to know that they're 'real.'

Nothing ruins a nice dinner like finding out that your food contains fictional ingredients. "I can't eat this! It's eight percent Flubber!"

90

Given the American psyche, I'm sure there will be the inevitable backlash, when it becomes hip and trendy to eat as badly as possible. Americans will be all over it.

After all, people bought Jolt Cola ("All the sugar, twice the caffeine"). Who's to say you won't start seeing chips advertised with *extra* salt?

Or maybe Dunkin' Donuts will start *adding* trans-fats to their pastries. You'll be able to order a hot dog and say, "Heavy on the nitrites, please!"

My Dinner with Marjoram

In my first couple years of cooking, I've been willing to experiment with almost anything on the shelf. Granted, my relationship with coriander isn't as close as we'd like, and I've only flirted with bay leaves, but in general, I've always tried to be even-handed in my spice-ifying.

I once used sage in a dish *simply* because I *hadn't* used it for a few weeks (turns out it doesn't work very well on ice cream). My point is that a cook should stay on good terms with *all* the herbs and spices in the pantry, and not become too attached to any of them.

Which is why I was taken aback the other day, while reaching for the rosemary. *Behind* the rosemary, in the back, with no label and a cap that had never been removed, I saw a container of marjoram.

I also realized that over the last two years, in preparing hundreds of dishes, I have never used marjoram.

**LOOKING AT THIS, I REALIZE I MAY HAVE
SMOKED A LOT OF MARJORAM IN COLLEGE**

While I was fawning over flashier jars, I was ignoring something that was considered downright **medicinal** by Hippocrates.

And according to *some* historical botanists (botanical historians?) the 'hyssop' referred to in the Passover story was actually marjoram!

Not impressed yet? Well, marjoram was also name-dropped by Shakespeare in Sonnet 99: *"And buds of marjoram had stol'n thy hair . . .*

Which, out of context, makes it sound like marjoram is some sort of depilatory. It's not, I'm pretty sure.

I couldn't call myself a cook until I had used everything on my rack at least a few times. But I need to feel comfortable with a new ingredient, so we arranged to meet.

At the start of the interview, I must say that marjoram was a bit defensive, but as we talked more, she loosened up.

Unfortunately, all audio from the interview was lost, so I've had to reconstruct the conversation from memory.

THE EXCLUSIVE INTERVIEW

"Before we get started…what would you prefer to be called? Can I call you Marj?"

> "That's fine . . . Just don't call me oregano. It's *really* irritating how often people mix us up – sure, we're the same *genus* but c'mon, we're ENTIRELY DIFFERENT SPECIES!
>
> Anyway, I'm *obviously* milder and sweeter than oregano. The only thing we have in common is the antioxidant thing, and that'll be passé soon."

"You've made it clear that you want to distance yourself from your cousin, but isn't it true that oregano used to be known as 'wild marjoram?'

Aren't you, in fact, trying to have it both ways? Isn't it your plan that, if someone runs out of oregano, they'll reach for *you* instead?"

> "That's outrageous! Look, I've always been open about my family. I don't deny that my *legal* name is *'Origanum marjorana,'* but that's not how I define *myself*.
>
> After all, I'm also a member of the mint family, and some people say I remind them of thyme. These are all just labels. Do we really mean anything?"

"Well, actually we -- need the labels so we know what's in the different jars –"

"But do we ever *really* know what's in *any* jar? Nobody knew I could talk, because nobody cared. Well now I'm giving an interview! I don't hear oregano talking!"

"On a less...confrontational note, how long have you been in the seasoning game? I know you've been around since at least 2008, because that's when I got most of my spices. But I understand you've been around longer than that, am I right?"

"First, let me correct you. I'm an herb, not a spice. A lot of us are, we just get stuck with the spices because nobody makes an 'herb rack.'

As to your question, lemme just say that, in ancient Egypt, I was used to appease the gods during embalming. THE GODS THEMSELVES, I TELL YOU! Anyway – yeah, I've been around a while."

"Many people believe you have healing powers, and it's said that you can cure dozens of conditions from sleep apnea to tonsillitis to anxiety, in addition to assuaging grief and deflecting bad luck. Do you support these outlandish claims?"

"Look, I may be a plant, but I'm not stupid. Of course I can't cure somebody's tonsillitis. I was *just* talking with my friend Rosemary about these whack-job aromatherapy people."

"I think it all started with one loony-tune herbalist in the sixteenth century, who claimed that smelling me "mundifieth the brayne." Not that some people couldn't benefit from a little brain mundifying . . .

So I'm not claiming to be medicinal, alright? I *will* say that if you use me as part of a nice rub on some leg of lamb, *that* might cure a lot of your ills. Oh, and if you find me on top of a grave, the dead person is guaranteed a good afterlife. That one's true."

"Some would say that you're too sensitive, and that may have led to your image problem. How do you respond?"

"I don't think I'm overly sensitive. Sure, I don't do well with frost, or even cold, and I prefer well-drained soil, but who doesn't? And I really need full sun exposure. And, I need a lot of room to spread out. Other than that, I think I'm pretty laid back."

"Let's get back to the subject of cooking. At the moment, you're thought of as an unusual spice, but you've been popular in the past. How do you plan on regaining your popularity?"

"If people knew how versatile I am, we wouldn't have to have this discussion."

"Trying French cooking? There's a little thing called *herbes de Provence* that you can't even DO without me.

Feeling like sausage? Hell, in Germany I'm *known* as the 'sausage spice.' I know I'm an herb, but you can't tell the Germans *anything*. And if you're into British food, you can always try me with goose and chestnuts.

Just . . . try me on something. Please. I'm getting desperate. At least try me in some meatloaf, would ya?"

There you have it. A revealing, even heartbreaking look at one herb's fight for respect. But on a deeper level, isn't marjoram speaking for all of us?

That's Not Really Food

I have accumulated a small library of weird old books, mostly from thrift stores, and was delighted to remember some vintage cookbooks in my collection. I thought I'd look through them for some ideas.

After all, it's not like food has changed much in the last hundred years. We eat pretty much the same stuff our grandparents did, right? It's just the technology that's changed, right?

When I looked at my 1927 Piggly Wiggly Cookbook, I had the idea to do a "Julie and Julia" sort of project, where I cook all the recipes in the book.

I didn't get much farther than the 'jellied chicken and oyster consommé.' That's wrong on so many levels. Jellied chicken . . . jellied anything in soup . . . chicken and oyster...

If that sounds like a big bowl of 'yikes,' how about 'pickled pigs feet'? That has the bonus of being both vile AND gelatinous!

Incidentally, the fact that something's 'pickled' doesn't offset the fact that you're eating feet. And 'codfish balls'? Write your *own* joke for that one.

I learned a few interesting things from the Piggly Wiggly Cookbook. For one, I learned that people in the twenties used something called Fluffo, which, as best I can tell, was whipped, aerated lard. I have a feeling *that* may have been the actual cause of the Great Depression.

I could see myself trying some of these 'vintage foods,' on a dare, or as a contestant on 'Fear Factor.' I won't be *cooking* any of them, and I probably won't see them as the 'special' at any restaurants I'm likely to visit.

But there are two things I *frequently* see on menus that I will avoid like . . . jellied chicken. Those would be eggplant and beef liver.

Eggplant would be fine, except for two things — its taste and its texture. I guess for most people, there is one food item that they not only don't enjoy, but actually don't *understand*. For me, it's eggplant.

You can try to trick me by adding other words *after* it like 'parmigiana' and 'catalana' and 'creole,' but at some point, I will get to the eggplant part, and I will *not* enjoy it.

There's even an 'eggplant recipe database' online with 3,116 recipes, or, as I refer to them, 'ways to disguise eggplant.'

As far as liver goes, let first admit an inconsistency. I have no problems with a little schmear of chicken liver on a sandwich. I have issues with a big slab of cow organ on a plate.

People will tell me, "You just haven't had liver the way *I* make it," to which I usually respond, "It's the organ that processes toxins out of the body. I'm pretty sure you're not supposed to eat it no matter *how* it's prepared."

If you're on a masochistic search for 'food' you're not supposed to eat, check out any State Fair. Every summer, hundreds of thousands of people stand in long lines in stifling heat for the opportunity to stuff their pieholes with items they would never eat outside the fairgrounds.

Usually this is because of humanity's strange obsession with food on a stick. I can't picture a restaurant *offering* deep-fried butter or chocolate-covered bacon on a plate for ten bucks, but put that crap on a stick, and we'll buy two of each!

I'd also like to take a moment to tell potential state fair vendors something: *enough* with the cheese. I like a smidge of gruyere as much as the next guy, but at last year's State Fair I think there was a booth selling cheese-filled cheese.

It's the weird combinations you find at a State Fair that bother me. Let me explain. Chocolate is good. Bacon is good. That doesn't mean chocolate and bacon are good *at the same time.*

I mean, sex is good, and bicycling is good, but I wouldn't recommend having sex ON a bicycle.Just stop screwing with the natural order of things. What's next -- beef soda?

How would you like to create the next trendy State Fair food item? It's easy -- just use this handy chart! First, choose one item from each column . . .

Column 1	Column 2
ALLIGATOR	SPAGHETTI
DUCK FAT	CHEDDAR CHEESE
BISON	BROCCOLI
BARBECUE BEEF	LICORICE
CHICKEN DUMPLINGS	ALMONDS
HOT DOGS	ORANGE MARMALADE
CAJUN PORK	ORZO
TROUT	MALTED MILK BALLS
JUMBO SHRIMP	JASMINE RICE
TURKEY DRUMSTICK	WASABI MUSTARD

Now use the two food items in any order, with one of the following phrases in between:
- "dipped in"
- "wrapped in"
- "stuffed with"

Then decide how to serve it:
- "on a stick"
- "in a cup."

Now, who wants Broccoli Stuffed Alligator On a Stick? Bring the kids to try some Trout Wrapped in Licorice! Even Grandma might try a cup of Almonds Dipped in Duck Fat!

There is one bizarre food hybrid that makes sense to me. I have to give credit to the visionaries at Domino's Pizza, who sell something called an 'Oreo pizza.' It's the size and shape of a pizza . . . and it's made out of Oreos.

This idea obviously came from someone in their marketing department who smokes pot, because only a stoner would think, "I really just want to eat a bunch of cookies, but I'd like to *pretend* I'm having an actual meal."

I Know It When I See It

If a picture is actually worth a thousand words, then I worked much harder than necessary on the book you're reading. This book has about forty thousand words, so by that formula, I could have simply taken forty pictures to make my point.

Having read more than my share of food blathering, and having now blathered a bit myself, I want to offer some suggestions to anyone out there considering getting all 'bloggy' about food:

> If you're writing about food, try to use words that at least, in some small, tangential way, relate to FOOD.

> Very few salads are actually *'ethereal'* (celestial; heavenly; of or pertaining to the upper regions of space), and please stop calling things 'TOOTHSOME.' That's like 'American Idol' judges saying something is 'pitchy' -- it doesn't mean anything!

> No matter how well your duck confit turned out, do not write that you had a *'foodgasm.'* I enjoy food.

> I've had some amazing meals in my life. *None* of them have been as good as sex. If you are in fact having 'foodgasms,' you need to see your doctor.

My next tip is for anyone who uses the subtle, nuanced medium of still photography to enhance their writing and communicate the essence of a dish:

Enough with the EXTREME CLOSEUPS! It's the photographic equivalent of YELLING! If I want to experience the 'essence' of a dish, I'll cook the freaking dish.

I don't need to see a picture that makes me feel like I've been miniaturized and trapped inside a freakishly large bowl of risotto. No matter how 'rustic' or 'artisanal' the risotto is.

I recently discovered that our camera has a special setting for 'food,' which tells me there are far too many people writing about food these days.

I'm not sure what the setting *does*, exactly, but I'm guessing that without it, none of my *pictures* of food would even *look like* food.

I've taken quite a few shots of things of things I've made in the kitchen. There are many things you could say about my photo-culinary skills, but you could never describe my pictures as 'food porn.'

The term 'food porn' was coined in the mid-eighties in the book *"Female Desire,"* and the author claimed,

"Cooking food and presenting it beautifully is an act of servitude...a symbol of a willing participation in servicing others."

I find the illustrations in 'Cook's Illustrated' as arousing as the next guy, but I have a fundamental problem with the phrase 'food porn.'

No matter how you define pornography, pictures of food do not qualify. It's true that the *words* used by food writers are straight out of 'Penthouse Forum.' Succulent . . . decadent . . . simmering. And don't forget all the drizzling and oozing.

THIS IS NOT AN EXAMPLE OF FOOD PORN

There's a simple question you must ask when debating whether food pictures can be pornographic -- would you be mortified if your mom walked in on you looking at a *picture of food?*

"Honey–I thought you blocked the Food Network in Bobby's room! The boy's DVR is filled with 'Iron Chef' episodes!

Next thing you know he'll be making...risotto!"

The term may be new, but the concept has been around for centuries. Take a look at this medieval obscenity, courtesy of Cristoforo Munari (1667-1720) –

"VASELLAME DI TERRACOTTA, ZUCCA, VERZA, SPALLA DI MAIALE E PIATTO CON COLTELLO PIATTI"
TRANSLATION: "STILL LIFE WITH UNFORTUNATELY-PLACED CABBAGE"

Or how this 1864 Monet, entitled, "The Joint of Meat"

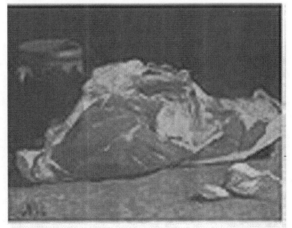

NOTICE HERE HOW MONET OBJECTIFIES HIS SUBJECT, TREATING IT AS IF IT WERE JUST "A PIECE OF MEAT"

I imagine that what's considered food porn varies depending on where you live. It's all about 'community standards.'

Maybe, in parts of the Deep South, a picture of a stick of butter is pornographic — maybe in the Ukraine, it's a soft-focus image of a bowl of borscht.

I like to take pictures of things that I write about, but I'm still learning. I don't always make a note of what the dish is being photographed, so those pictures tend to be useless ("I'm pretty sure that was another meatloaf, darlingbut I can't really tell.")

I also have a tendency to shoot pictures from directly above the dish, so I have some pictures of a cobbler that look more like aerial views of an archaeological dig site.

The Girlfriend typically takes the pictures, which I guess makes her my "food stylist.' We usually only take pictures of things that turned out well, but there have been exceptions.

I asked her to let me take one particularly moving picture of her holding a saucepan, so that I can, if necessary, remind her of the Tragic Tale of the Burnt Peas, the next time she offers to take over the cooking.

You Can Look It Up

Learning to cook requires learning a new language as well. It seems like there are dozens of terms for even the simplest kitchen tasks, and a lot of the words aren't even in English! As I started to cook more, I gathered more recipes online, and had to look up more words online.

I'm always a little nervous using Wikipedia because it's 'community edited,' which means anybody can change an entry. I hear it's better now, but I was always worried that I would try some technique from Wikipedia for making short ribs and accidentally create a crude explosive device.

I knew I had to stop relying on the internet when I read this entry for the word 'julienne':

ju·li·enne☐ ☐[joo-lee-en; Fr. zhy-lyen]

adjective (of food, especially vegetables) cut into the shape of sixties actress Julie Newmar (derived from 'Julie N.')

By now, I've mastered quite a few bits of cooking jargon, which I try to drop into the conversation. Some people are less impressed than others . . .

The Girlfriend: What's for dinner tonight?

Me: I blanched some *haricots verts* to go with the braised turkey, and right now I'm working on a remoulade.

The Girlfriend: Did you say we're having turkey?

There's no reason to memorize every arcane food word or phrase, but you should probably learn a handful of basic terms. Conveniently, I've assembled a sampling of cooking terms that I believe could cause some confusion for the novice cook.

Bear in mind, some of these refer to fairly advanced techniques or complicated dishes, so in certain case, I chose to simplify the definitions.

A COOK'S LEXICON

SOME DEFINITIONS MAY NOT BE 'TECHNICALLY' CORRECT, AND CERTAIN FOODS MENTIONED MAY NOT, IN FACT, EXIST.

Antipasto: *small, unsatisfying portions of food served before the meal, typically at tedious group events, designed to distract people from how long it's taking to get their main course*

Aspic: *a jellied meat stock, initially created as a prank that got out of hand...since it is a jellied meat stock, it is not meant for <u>actual</u> consumption*

Bard: *to tie fat around meat before cooking, in order to increase the amount of fat...also, to recite Shakespearean monologues while cooking*

Broiler: *the part of an oven, typically on the bottom, that is impossible to clean...most often used to test the smoke alarm in my apartment*

Brûlée: *from the French for 'burnt,' first used to illustrate that everything sounds more appetizing in French*

Burgoo: *a spicy stew, sometimes called 'roadkill soup,' popular in areas where people would willingly eat something called 'roadkill soup'*

Caul fat: *the fatty membrane surrounding an animal's internal organs, used in dishes that require a fatty organ-covering membrane*

Free range chicken: *any chicken that is allowed to roam outside of a cage before being slaughtered; these 'special chickens' are able to run errands, get library cards or take night classes...they can frequently be found taunting traditionally 'caged' chickens*

Mandolin: *a device used for cutting food into uniformly sized slices; often confused with 'mandolin,' a device used for creating bluegrass music; the first mandolins actually were used for both purposes*

Mince: *to finely chop something while watching 'Sex and the City'*

Parboil: *a combination of the words 'partially' and 'boil'... related words include 'almosteam' and 'sortapoach.'*

Proof (see also Prove): *in baking, the process of illustrating, through logic and deductive reasoning, that you should make cookies more often*

Reduce: *when referring to liquid in a pan or skillet, the step immediately before 'burn'*

Salamander: *a kitchen tool used by chefs to aid in browning meat; more frequently, a double entendre employed by chefs, as in, "Waitress, have you seen my salamander?"*

Sauerkraut: *A generally unhappy marriage of cabbage and bacteria, from the same people who brought us World War II*

Scotch egg: *the result of taking a hardboiled egg, wrapping it in sausage, coating it with bread crumbs, and then deep-frying; a technique designed to make something bad out of something healthy (see also 'Scotch broccoli')*

Tofu: *a tasteless, oddly-textured substance that allows vegans to believe that they don't miss real hot dogs*

Yam: *Apparently not the same as a sweet potato; best to avoid both just to be sure.*

But Could They Write A Recipe?

It's a little known fact that many famous authors, at one time or another, tried their hands at writing cookbooks. Recently discovered correspondence between these authors and their publishers reveal the culinary passion of some of history's most famous writers.

 *William Shakespeare*

Shakespeare mentioned food in many of his plays. In *'Romeo and Juliet,'* he offers the cooking mantra,
"'Tis an ill cook cannot lick his own fingers."

And in 'As You Like It," there's this classic food-related insult:
"Truly, you art damned like an ill-roasted egg, all on one saide" In *Henry IV, Part I*, Shakespeare introduces the phrase "eaten me out of house and home." At the end of *Part II*, King Henry has finally forgiven Hal and dies peacefully.

In the never-published *third* part of the saga (to be titled *Figs and Worts: Recipes for Martlemas*), we see Hal planning to abdicate the throne and open a chain of topless alehouses.

Charles Dickens

The problem Dickens faced when he started a cookbook wasn't with his recipe for pigeonpie. '*David Copperfield*' (the novel, not the annoying magician) hints at Dickens' love for cooking with a description that could easily have come from a judge on 'Chopped':

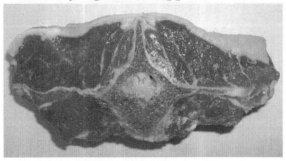

"The leg of mutton came up very red within, and very pale without; besides having a foreign substance of a gritty nature sprinkled over it, as if it had had a fall into the ashes of that remarkable kitchen fireplace."

No, the Dickens was never able to publish his cookbook was that he insisted on releasing his recipes in weekly segments.

With these 'cliffhangers', the first week you might get the ingredients, then the following week the actual instructions, and his publisher believed this could frustrate the amateur cook at home.

James Joyce

Like many English majors, I must have read at *least* three or four pages of Joyce's stream-of-consciousness classic, '*Ulysses*."

But publishers weren't as thrilled with Joyce's intended follow-up. This excerpt from '*Ulysses*' was originally to be the introduction to his **"*Portrait of the Cook as a Young Man.***'

> "*If you leave a bit of codfish for instance. I could see the bluey silver over it. Night I went down to the pantry in the kitchen. Don't like all the smells in it waiting to rush out.*"

e. e. cummings

Buoyed by the success of his poem '*[as freedom is a breakfastfood]*,' cummings wanted to do an entire book of breakfast recipes written in his idiosyncratic style.

However, an early edition of "*breakthefastwithsome eggs maybe and a heartywarmmuffin*" proved to be unpopular with cooks accustomed to punctuation.

Raymond Chandler

Chandler may be known for murder and deception, but at heart he was a foodie. He began work on his cookbook in 1956, but only a few snippets of it have survived.

Apparently, the book was to be called *"Easy Chow for Dames and Grifters,"* and in it, Chandler demonstrates a fondness for hearty American fare, while still maintaining his uniquely hard-boiled writing voice.

This is a fragment of one of Raymond Chandler's unpublished recipes:

> *"Start the marinade early, when the moon is exhausted and the sunlight still has the deluded notion that it can fight its way through the choking L.A. smog. Sautee the onions until they're as transparent as a philandering husband's alibi.*
>
> *Then take your knife, glistening like the drop of sweat on the forehead of a guy who just bet his last hundred on a longshot at the track, and cut the lamb.*
>
> *The oven needs to be hotter than an off-the-shoulder silk gown wrapped around the curves of a sultry chanteuse, but not as hot as the asphalt on Wilshire Boulevard in July."*

And this cryptic instruction: *"Cook on middle rack for 40-45 minutes."*

Jay McInerny

The first hints at what would become McInerny's iconic style occur in a small volume he pitched to publishers in early 1983.

Entitled "Bright Lights, Big Flavor!," the manuscript is filled with all the touchstones that marked McInerny's later work, starting with the urban-angsty, ironic second-person detachment of the opening:

> *"You're tired and, beat down but you know you have to cook. You find yourself in a messy kitchen, trying to make sense of the instructions on the package. You think to yourself, "Why did I buy orzo?"*
>
> *You realize the orzo was a mistake, just like the eight-ball you got from Rico at the club. But you're depressed, and you still need to eat something, anything to take the edge off.*
>
> *Your hands are shaking and your head feels like a construction site, so you resign yourself to a morning bowl of orzo and regret."*

Publishers felt that McInerny overemphasized cocaine as a seasoning, and recipes like 'Peruvian marching powdered biscuits' ensured a fairly narrow audience.

Dr. Seuss

While the venerable Theodore Geisel earned accolades as a children's writer, he hoped one day to publish a cookbook for more adult palettes.

To be called "Oh, the Couscous You Will Cookcook," no book deal happened, as Geisel's publisher worried that someone trying his recipes would become confused trying to find whimsical ingredients such as "floopers," "jibberjam," and "cardamom."

You Should Hear the Zucchini

Imagine a musical ensemble that makes all of its own instruments a few hours before every concert. Or, imagine if performance art broke out at a farmers market. Or, maybe there's no way to describe the Vienna Vegetable Orchestra . . .

Sometimes called 'Das Erste Wiener Gemüseorchester, they play music on instruments made from fresh fruits and vegetables.

PHOTOGRAPH TAKEN WITH SPECIAL LENS THAT FILTERS OUT JOY

The twelve member ensemble composes and plays a wildly eclectic mix of modern music including "beat-oriented House tracks, experimental Electronic, Free Jazz, Noise, Dub..." Oddly, enough, they don't mention 'bluegrass,' which would seem to be right up their alley.

They take about ninety pounds of fresh produce for each concert (playing concert halls across Europe), then a few hours before showtime they make their instruments. Cutting, carving, chopping, drilling–you know, the usual pre-concert preparation . . .

Carrot flutes, eggplant clappers, and celeriac bongos; and radish horns and pepper rattles and cucumberphones (Dr. Seuss again!) and of course the leek violin. If I'd only listened when my parents pressured me to take 'leek violin' lessons.

Unfortunately, a group this . . . cutting edge has been interviewed before, and all the good, 'real' questions have already been asked (*damn you NPR!*). But if I really wanted to play cub reporter, I would have to put aside my skepticism and my preconceptions.

For instance, despite what you might have learned from "The Sound of Music," not all Austrian performers are like the Von Trapp family and on the run from Nazis. So there goes that story angle.

Were they a bunch of pretentious, bored young Austrian intellectuals with too much free time? Because historically, *that's* led to some problems.

To get to know the group better, their publicist put me in touch with Jörg Piringer, and he proved to be affable, if a bit serious (I know, you wouldn't think a dude who plays cucumberphone would be serious).

He was also very tolerant when I told him – in German -- how glad I was to talk with him. Although it's been a lot of years, so it's also possible that I said, "That building is very tall." Anyway, on to the interview . . .

I thought I would break the ice with something goofy, try to loosen him with distinctly silly question. So, I asked him if the Vegetable Orchestra would consider collaborating with a non-vegetable-playing musician –

"We have worked with a trumpet player."

Well, now we're off to a rollicking start. Maybe he just hadn't gotten comfortable with me yet. Then I suggested the group could tour with Lady Gaga (she wears a meat dress, they play vegetables -- it's a balanced concert!), but that idea didn't seem to grab him either.

The orchestra was formed in 1998, and the top-selling music act that year was Celine Dion, so I asked whether they were trying to make a statement when they started,   as a response to Celine' style of mainstream pop music --

"We're more concerned with contemporary classical music."

And here, I was hoping for a little Celine-bashing. I pressed on, though, convinced that somehow I would find the *right* stupid question to break through his European exterior and maybe get the Austrian equivalent of a *laugh* out of him.

I was fascinated by the notion of how a group like this gets started. I wanted to know whether anyone in the ensemble had *prior* vegetable or produce-related experience, he said,

"Not really, only cooking. Not really playing, or anything like that."

So, I guess they were just having dinner one night, and someone said "I wonder what sound this would make if I blew into it."

Still trying to stir up a something, I asked him if there would be tension in the group if one of the members formed an all-*meat* band as a side project:

"Nobody would have a problem with that . . . everybody has other projects, because the Vegetable Orchestra isn't big enough . . . it doesn't provide enough income for everybody."

I stopped and reflected on that. What kind of world is this, where people can't make an honest living as vegetable musicians?

You can't interview a musician without talking about groupies, so I asked Jörg if their groupies were typically vegans, and he said, *"Not really,"* but he also said they get a lot of *"feedback"* from vegans, and that's some sort of slang.

But then he tried to tell me the Orchestra doesn't *have* groupies, and I don't buy it. He might play vegetables, but they're still *musicians* who *tour*. They get laid plenty.

I was becoming desperate to uncover a scandal, so I asked Jörg how *stoned* they were when they came up with the idea for a vegetable orchestra, and he actually told me,

"We were just crazy with ideas."

Yeah, and I'm just high on life. Speaking of the munchies, the orchestra has recently stopped what had been a tradition at their shows – making a soup from their instruments and sharing it with their audience. Apparently some venues suggested that might not be a great idea, hygiene-wise.

I saved the two most important questions for last. The first one had an obvious answer, but it was nice to have a professional musician validate what I've said for years: What's the best-sounding vegetable? "*Broccoli*".

My last question had to be great. I couldn't waste an opportunity to ask a cutting-edge musician at the vanguard of the new music scene the kind of question that gets to the heart of his creative passion: Do Brussels sprouts *sound* better than they *taste*?

"Well, you can make some squeaking sounds if you press them together . . . and I like the taste!"

As it turned out, my gourd-wielding friend was an incredibly good sport about my unorthodox questions, and as much as I may have initially intended to mock the Vienna Vegetable Orchestra, I listened to the music, and, to be honest, I thought it was pretty groovy.

You let yourself get caught up in these oddly resonant, earthy sounds, layered on a bed of rhythms banged out on pumpkins and gourds...the leafy greens keeping time...it's actually really good. And it's good *for* you!

It's not mainstream, assembly-line accessible, but if you can open your ears to it, 'vegetable music' can be pretty tasty. I think if they really want a foothold in the U.S, though, they should put out an album of covers. Of songs with food in the title. I bet they could do a killer version of Booker T.'s *'Green Onions.'*

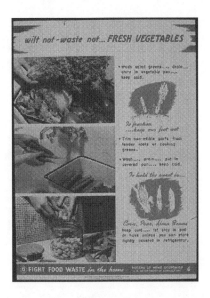

IT WAS A SIMPLER TIME, BEFORE PEOPLE USED VEGETABLES TO CREATE AVANT-GARDE CHAMBER MUSIC

A Culinary Soundtrack

Music and food have been intertwined for centuries. In fact, one of the greatest operatic composers, Gioachino Rossini, was such a gourmand that not only did he compose some of his most famous arias *while* dining, but several dishes are named in his honor.

In fact, the term 'Alla Rossini' usually refers to any dish incorporating truffles, foie gras, and a demi-glace sauce. So thankfully, I now know what to call all those truffle and fois gras dishes I cook.

Rossini even wrote several piano pieces *about* food, including his 'Four Hors D'oeuvres.' If you get a chance to hear it, listen to the touching second movement, 'Les Anchois,' undoubtedly the finest piece of music ever composed about anchovies.

For some reason, early in the twentieth century, it was popular to name foods after opera singers. The next time you dig into some Turkey Tetrazzini, you can thank Luisa Tetrazzini, the Italian soprano.

And a rival of Tetrazzini, Australian diva Nellie Melba, inspired Escoffier to create Peach Melba *and* Melba Toast.

"GREAT. NOW WHEN PEOPLE HEAR MY NAME, THEY'LL THINK OF INEDIBLE DRY BREAD"

In today's music scene, I suppose great chefs are naming dishes after hip-hop stars, but I'm not sure the food world is ready for Eggs *Kanye*, *Wu-Tang* Chicken, or Lake Trout *a la Snoop*

"Place butter and chronic in a medium sizzlepizzle"...

Since I like to listen to music while I'm cooking, I went searching for some songs *about* food. I tried to be strict about my criteria. The song has to be *about* the food.

For instance, 'Mayonnaise' by Smashing Pumpkins isn't included, because it has nothing whatsoever to do with mayonnaise. And because Billy Corgan has always annoyed me.

Also, I had to leave out Warrant's 'Cherry Pie,' because apparently it is not about an *actual* cherry pie.

I thought I'd struck gold with the Talking Heads album 'More Songs About Buildings and Food,' but it turns out the album includes NO songs about buildings OR food.

Lastly, I tried not to use any songs that suck. For example, the 1947 Mel Tormé abomination "Tacos, Enchiladas, and Beans," made popular by Doris Day, which features lyrical gems like

You're the only one my heart adores
You've only got three competitors
    Tacos, enchiladas, and beans
and this
    Love 'em, dozens of 'em
    I consume them by the score

126

The farthest back I went for my playlist was the 1930s; the most recent track is from 1983. This list may not work for everyone – you might prefer to julienne to the Jayhawks, or need a little Morrissey in your *mise en place.*

But I've put together a pretty eclectic mix. It's best to start safe, with songs *explicitly* about food, if you're not used to mixing music with cooking.

The fact that you like Sarah McLachlan doesn't mean her music is the right background for your dinner 'pre-show.' You might just become too depressed to finish, and end up slumped over the counter thinking of sad puppies.

So grab these tunes off the interwebs, or from the clouds, or however the hell kids get their music these days. Then take whatever iGadget you have, use the playlist on the next two pages, and start cooking.

Note: The first three tracks are instrumentals, and while I suppose that means they're not technically 'about' food, I think they each capture the spirit of the foods after which they're named.

Herb Alpert and the Tijuana Brass
"Whipped Cream" (1965)
> Just try to forget that this was also the theme to the 'The Dating Game.'

Booker T. and the MGs
"Green Onions" (1962)
> I don't think this song would be nearly as cool if it were called 'Scallions.' I don't know why.

Dizzy Gillespie All Stars
'Salt Peanuts' (1942)
> The be-bop rhythms should make tedious prep work a snap.

Fats Waller
'All That Meat and No Potatoes'   (1936)
> A cautionary tale of the dangers of poor meal planning...

Slim Gaillard
"Matzoh Balls" (1939)
> Historic, as it may have been the first recorded use of the word 'matzoh' by anyone named 'Slim.'

Nat 'King' Cole
'Frim Fram Sauce'   *(1945)*

There is no such thing as 'frim fram sauce,' but there certainly should be.

Louis Jordan
"Beans and Cornbread" (1949)

Just your basic jump-blues chat between a pot of beans...and some cornbread. They work it out in the end.

Hank Williams
"Jambalaya"   *(1952)*

In probably the *least* definitive cover version ever, the Carpenters did their version of this on their album *'Now and Then.'* I should not know that.

Tom Waits
"Eggs and Sausage" (1976)

Sometimes, you need to go to the local greasy spoon with the other nighthawks if you want a decent meal.

ZZ Top
"TV Dinners" (1983)

In case you decide, "Screw it, I don't feel like cooking *or* going out." It's not especially deep, but it's redeemed by the line "twenty-year old turkey in a thirty-year old tin."

All the Music You Can Eat

British author and philosopher G.K. Chesterton once said, "Music with dinner is an insult both to the cook and the violinist." Coincidentally, an anonymous violinist in London once said, "Screw Chesterton. I wouldn't invite him over for dinner anyway."

Me—I love music with dinner. I just don't want it to *overshadow* the food, like I'm at a Hard Rock Cafe.Did you know that there are a hundred and fifty Hard Rock Cafes around the world?

I wonder if at some point, they're gonna expand **too** much, open a new location, and realize too late that they're out of the really cool rock memorabilia. They'll have to display things like Mick Jagger's dry cleaning ticket, or a guitar used by the guy who sang harmony for Air Supply.

Back to music and food. I'm always looking for ways to combine my two passions, and as I was listening to some random playlist the other day, I decided to create a menu using only foods that are *also* the names of chart-topping recording artists.

I was strict about it—the name of the group or artist, by itself, had to be something you could actually eat or drink—no '*Smashing* Pumpkins,' or 'Strawberry *Alarm Clock.*'

And I was a little sad to find out there's no such thing as 'April Wine,' because that meant I had to exclude one of the hardest rocking bands ever to come from Nova Scotia.

I threw together a three-course meal based on only these acts—twelve recording artists who, between them, sold millions of singles and albums, and together, would make a damned fine dinner.

Note: 'Singles' were individual songs you could buy in a physical store, and 'albums' were entire collections of songs by the same artist, all pressed into slabs of vinyl you could hold in your hand.

You had to use a special device to access the songs called a 'record player,' and you had to listen to the songs in the order the artist intended. It's hard to believe how primitive music was then.

APPETIZER

Hot Tuna on Bread with Hot Butter

We whet our appetites by remembering a band that oozed out of the musical lava lamp of late sixties San Francisco. Hot Tuna's first album hit #30 on the charts in 1970.

Here I've paired the patchouli-scented Jefferson Airplane side project with the relentlessly bland stylings of Bread (Thirteen 'Hot 100' singles between 1970 and 1977?! How did we let *that* happen?).

Don't forget the Hot Butter, and believe me, if you've ever heard their #9 hit from 1972, 'Popcorn,' you'll remember it. And if you do, you've probably got it stuck in your head right now. Sorry.

> *For this open-faced appetizer, try sautéing the tuna in some herb butter, and by herb, I mean marijuana.*
>
> *Your house will reek for a few hours, but you'll be tripping to some psychedelic blues, so it won't matter, and why are you trying to harsh my buzz, anyway, man?*
>
> *Wait, is someone at the door? Are you a narc?*

MAIN COURSE

Salt and Pepa Meatloaf
Black-eyed Peas, Red Hot Chili Peppers

Sure, he descended into self-parody on 'Celebrity Apprentice,' but let's remember that Meat Loaf's 1977 opus, "Bat out of Hell," went *fourteen* times platinum, which represents fourteen gazillion records sold!

Unfortunately it also spawned *"Paradise by the Dashboard Light,"* which has inspired frat boys and their girlfriends the world over to try to 'perform' the song at karaoke.

Any good meatloaf needs some seasoning, so we'll add the best-selling female rap act of all-time, with Salt and Pepa releasing six platinum singles between '86 and '97.

Finally, combine black-eyed peas (over sixty million records sold since '03) with chili peppers (five Top Five albums), and you've got a big helping of quasi-funk, right there. It's like having a near-funk experience.

> *For the meatloaf, you can find a kajillion recipes online, but, I rely on a handful of very old, musty, tattered ACTUAL cookbooks. You know, made out of paper, like in olden tymes.*

Here's a meatloaf recipe from a 1914 collection put out by the Boston alumnae chapter of Alpha Phi.

There doesn't seem to be anything particularly 'Swedish' about it, and notice that there's no middle ground as far as the onion is concerned—two thin slices, or just shove the whole onion in.

Swedish Loaf

Two pounds lower round, one and one-half cups bread crumbs, one egg, salt, pepper, onion if liked, milk to moisten. Pass meat through chopper. Beat egg into mixing bowl and mix thoroughly with meat, salt and pepper. Add alternately bread crumbs and milk, stirring constantly so that the whole may be thoroughly moistened. The success of this dish depends upon the thoroughness with which the ingredients are blended. If an onion flavor is relished, chop two slices fine and add, or place whole onion in roasting pan. Mould mixture in shape of roast in pan, place butter in corners and roast one hour, basting frequently Serve with brown or tomato sauce.

GRACE POTTER BELISLE, ex-'99.

In honor of the singer, be really loud and dramatic when you cook this meatloaf.

Cook the black-eyed peas until al dente. Just before the beans are done, finely shave a few chili peppers into a hot skillet.

Add cooked beans to skillet. Stir frequently. Sprinkle grated parmesan cheese and kosher salt on top of entire mixture in skillet. Serve hot.

DESSERT

Ambrosia, Raspberries and Cranberries
Vanilla Fudge with Cream
"Cake"

Ambrosia can be a little too sweet for some tastes, but they did have five Top 40 singles between 1975 and 1980. Someone must like it.

I figure we'll balance that with a little tartness from the Cranberries (a little yelpy for my tastes, but four Top Twenty albums) and the Raspberries, who, from 1970-75, featured Eric Carmen, before he decided to craft a solo career of mopey self-absorbed treacle.

Beginning in 1967, Vanilla Fudge released eight albums and reached #6 on the U.S. charts with a slow, proto-grunge, ultimately creepy cover of the Supremes' "You Keep Me Hanging On."

Top that with some Cream (1966-1970), you get two more Top Ten hits, and the only million-selling album in history named after Benjamin Disraeli.

Lastly, we serve up a little alt-indie-postmodern rock with Cake. Between 1996 and 2011, they've had five albums debut in the top fifty, so looking and sounding bored must sell. If you really want to end the meal with a hipster's sensibility, serve something that isn't cake, but still call it "cake."

Since not as many people make 'ambrosia' any more (or listen to them), here's another recipe from the 1927 Piggly Wiggly Cookbook.

Ambrosia, Southern Style

1 can Baker's Southern Style Coco-   1 to 2 cups pineapple
   nut   2 bananas
4 to 6 oranges   (Optional)

   Cut sections of oranges into about three pieces, add diced banana and diced or shredded pineapple. Sweeten to taste. Add coconut and serve cold. Delightful variations can be made with any seasonable fruit, as peaches, pears, cherries and strawberries.

Sadly, Miss Belisle and the Class of 1899 graduated fifteen years before the first Piggly Wiggly Store opened, or I'm sure they would have served this.

Just be sure to use Baker's Southern Style Coconut (none of that Arctic-style coconut), and remember—just like in life, bananas are optional.

BEVERAGES

Hot Chocolate with Sugarcubes

Mmm . . . Hot Chocolate. Although mostly known here for the disco earworm "You Sexy Thing," in the U.K. they had a Top 100 chart hit every year between 1970 and 1984. Even *they're* not sure why.

Toss in some Sugarcubes, and you'll have an Icelandic group with three Top Twenty albums, featuring a quirky, young, swan-obsessed girl named Björk Guðmundsdóttir.

I wouldn't recommend playing all of these artists for your background music during this dinner. That would be far too obvious, and you'd have to actually listen to Bread. Here's an alternative:

Isaac Hayes
'Hot Buttered Soul'
1969

None of the four tracks on this album have anything to do with food, but Hayes' twelve-minute version of the Bacharach-David classic 'Walk on By' should pair nicely with the appetizers, and by the time everyone starts to feel the groove of "'Hyperbolicsyllabicsesquedalymistic," nobody will care if your meatloaf isn't quite perfect.

Fear, Loathing, and Porridge

If I told you I knew a chef who has created the most decadent and exquisite porridge from locally sourced ingredients, full of sublime flavors and textures, would you think that this chef:

A)   Trained for years at Le Cordon Bleu in France, is probably named 'Jean-Michel,' and might be a little snooty

B) Trained at a flapjack house in Ada, Oklahoma, dropped acid "a lot," was stabbed at a Van Halen concert, likes to "blow fire just for kicks," owns a herd of buffalo, and has a tattoo that was hand-drawn by Hunter S. Thompson's illustrator.

If you answered 'B,' then you must know Mitch Omer, co-owner and executive chef at *Hell's Kitchen*, who has been following his mischievous and sometimes destructive muse for thirty-five years.

CHEF MITCH OMER INSTRUCTING HIS STAFF IN THE FINE POINTS OF PROPER FIRE SAFETY TECHNIQUES

We sat down to chat in a booth toward the back of his restaurant, and when our server came by, I couldn't help but thinking, "It must suck to have your boss seated in your section."

A few things on the menu jumped out at me, and most of those involved bison. There's bison sausage...there's even a bison 'Sausage *Bread*,' which I guess is for people who just don't have the time to eat their sausage and bread *separately*.

I ordered the Bison Benedict and a Bloody Mary. And I hate to say this, Wheaties people, but *that's* your 'breakfast of champions'. There's nothing like biting into a hunk of majestic buffalo to give you that 'top-of -the-food-chain' feeling.

Meat is a big part of the menu here, and a fairly generic question about foie gras (which he keeps at home but doesn't serve in the restaurant) led to this . . . passionate response:

> "I'm sorry -- I don't give a fuck -- its great! They been doin this for what —centuries?
>
> Look, if we can get free range, great, but . . . they're bred to be killed."

My vegan readers will probably be quite upset by all of this, but thankfully, due to their meat-free diet, they won't have the strength to write me an angry letter.

The first thing you notice when you enter the basement restaurant / bar / music venue known as *Hell's Kitchen* is the decor.

Thankfully, unlike a lot of basement restaurant / bar / music venues, the decor isn't just a tease–the food is as good (and as interesting) as the art.

Specifically, the art of Ralph Steadman, who has drawn iconic caricatures since the days when *Rolling Stone* was actually counter-culture. He may be best known for illustrating the drug and booze-fueled narratives of *'Fear and Loathing in Las Vegas.'*

The walls at *Hell's* are covered in Steadman's dark, bold lines, including an original called 'Big Head #5.' And Mitch Omer has *two* Steadmans inked on his right arm, one of them autographed.

Now, I don't think I have *ever* been such a big fan of someone that I would have had their work *burned into my flesh*. Probably just as well, because my tastes in music weren't very adventurous when I was younger, and I wouldn't want to have to explain a tattoo of John Denver.

Talking about Steadman naturally led us to Hunter S. Thompson *("his stuff was a Bible for me in the seventies")*, so I asked Mitch to improvise a sandwich in Hunter's name that would be suitably 'gonzo' –

"You gotta start with a decent bread, gotta look at a focaccia, or something like that, and then . . . I'd just put some mayonnaise and Vicodin in and wash it down with some scotch, make it like a French dip and . . . you dip the fucker in *scotch*. So there you go, you got the Thompson Dip."

Mitch spent some time working concert security (hence the aforementioned stabbing), but instead of making him jaded, he seems wistfully nostalgic about his ass-kicking past.

That same past, and a concerned roommate, led him, oddly enough, to try LSD . . .

"I was working as a bouncer during this time, **and** I started working third shift as a baker. I'd kick the shit out of bikers through the night, and roll in dough until the morning.

I was fighting every night and absolutely loving it. My roommate told me one night that he was afraid I was going to kill one of these bastards, and well, 'this might mellow you out a little bit.'

I was still tripping on acid one day before work. It was wild; the dough was convulsing, the colors on the walls were running, and I had to take very slow, deep breaths to keep it under control.

It was cool, but I would never let that happen again. I wasn't giving my employer my best work, and I'm all about quality. I'll just stick to pot."

And of course, as any aspiring pastry chef knows, you always have to work with the dough until it completely stops 'convulsing.'

I knew that Mitch wasn't exactly a fan of celebrity-chef culture, *and* since *he* brought up fighting, I asked who would win if he fought celebrity chef Anthony Bourdain.

Bourdain, of course, has fashioned himself as somethin of a bad-ass (of course, how much of a bad-ass can you be when you're featured on the Travel Channel?). So, who wins?

> "That's actually a good question. I've met Bourdain. He's 6'5", and I'm 6'4" , and he's younger than me by a ways, so he's got that going for him . . .
>
> What I've got going for *me* is a history of fighting."

In addition to fighting random goons at rock shows, Mitch Omer has had to battle himself. He talks (almost proudly) about 'finally' being diagnosed with bipolar disorder, and seems at peace with who he is now.

And if obsessive-compulsive disorder ever had a telethon, Mitch could be its spokesman. He actually sent his book, *'Damn Good Food–157 Recipes From Hell's Kitchen' back* to the publisher on first printing.

That's because it had 156 recipes, and he doesn't like *even numbers* (readers with OCD will appreciate this, once they're done counting the number of words in the preceding paragraph).

Mitch also acknowledged that his OCD can be an asset in the kitchen:

"Oh, God yes! When I'm cooking, I'm dialed in. And if I go into the walk-in, and that shit isn't the way I want it, with the handles turned that way, or if anything's not facing forward, with labels, and dated. I've actually had the health department take photographs, for their training."

"ASK ME ANYTHING YOU WANT!"

What music do you listen to when you're cooking?

"It's gotta be movin' . . . Led Zeppelin, or Allman Brothers off the first two albums, because you lose Berry Oakley and Duane Allman it's not the Allman Brothers. Or blues -- electric slide blues, someone like Sonny Boy Williamson."

What was the first meal you cooked for someone important to you?"

"A chateaubriand I made for my mom and dad."

What's your favorite utensil?

> "Fuckin' knives! I've got a couple of gems in my office, and I've got some surgical tools."
> *(which included a bizarre finger-amputation doohickey that looked like a cross between a cigar-clipper and a gun. It was comforting to remember that he doesn't drop acid anymore).*

If you had a time machine, where and when would you like to have cooked?

> "Fifteenth century Italy. When Catherine De' Medici left Italy to go to France, she took her whole retinue with her, including her retinue of cooks.
>
> They felt the French were coarse, backward people, and she was NOT gonna eat that food. So the Italians came with all their talents, and they *trained* the French chefs.
>
> Now France is known as this gastronomic capital. They owe every fuckin' bit of that to Catherine De' Medici. She invented high heels . . . Jesus Christ, she did everything! She was a great chick -- she took a bunch of knuckle-dragging Neanderthals and taught 'em how to cook."

NOTE: SHE WAS ALSO A TYRANT RESPONSIBLE FOR
THE MASSACRE OF THOUSANDS OF HUGUENOTS.

Would you put a gourmet spin on the classic Minnesota 'hotdish?'

"Fuck that! These guys do that, take classic food and 'deconstruct' it — 'Oh, we're doing it with some different cheese or we're doing it with homemade this and this or whatever,' and I'm like, that isn't it!

Wanna talk comfort food? Go down to Winona and talk to the women there that do the funerals. Every time somebody dies, they get the call....they bring hot dish—that's what they do! And they're not using venison, or, my God, heirloom tomatoes. Fuck that.

I mentioned the porridge, and I'm not alone. Senator Al Franken's a fan, and Nora Ephron. It's a concoction of maple syrup, blueberries, craisins, hazelnuts, heavy cream and Native American hand-parched wild rice, and it's also a great lesson in commitment.

When Hell's Kitchen opened almost a decade ago (that's three hundred years in restaurant time), people weren't buying the porridge.

They also weren't buying his shrimp and grits (*"NOBODY fuckin' bought it–I mean NOBODY!"*), which might have been because, as Mitch puts it, *"It's the Midwest — nobody knows what a grit is."*

He eventually gave up on the grits, but he believed in the porridge, at one point giving it away to get people to try it.

Now, thanks to the same business model my pot dealer uses, Mitch's porridge *"has taken on a life of its own."*

I learned a lot in the hour I spent with Mitch. For instance, if you want pecans in your cinnamon rolls, you should sautée them first in a pan with salt and butter.

Then you add them to the dough *after* it rises, or else your nuts will be mealy (and how many meals have we all had that were ruined by mealy nuts?).

Oh, and I learned that bear meat is *"stupid lean"* and *"sweeter than venison."*

I mentioned to him that it seems every time I 'create' something, I discover that a hundred thousand amateur chefs with internet connections came up with the same idea. He told me,

> "Look, it's like our lemon ricotta pancakes. I don't remember ever *hearing* about lemon ricotta pancakes, I just remember thinking 'I want to put some lemon and ricotta in a goddam pancake!'
>
> Bottom line is we *did* create these things, and if a million other people created the same thing, big deal!"

Coolest moment for me: when I told him about my special turkey burgers (with maple syrup in the middle of the patty), and he said, *"I would have never thought of doing that."* I chose to take that as a compliment.

That led to his homemade maple-bison sausage, and then we were talking about the smells that come off the grill from the sugars breaking down, and suddenly we were just a couple of cooks, swapping stories about caramelization.

Cooking With Testosterone

Here's how I know that I'm not a traditional alpha male: the idea of grilling does NOTHING for me. I simply do not have the 'barbecue gene' in my DNA. I'm fairly certain I have the 'show tunes gene,' but that's rarely needed at a backyard picnic.

Sure, I enjoy the taste of barbecued meat, but I have no interest in creating it. *Anthropologically*, I get it. The whole 'primal flashback to killing a wooly mammoth and throwing its carcass onto an open fire' thing. But the deal is, human society has evolved, and now we can cook INDOORS.

The problem I have with the 'primal' argument for grilling's appeal is that most people who throw slabs of dead animal on the fire didn't hunt and kill the animal themselves. *(Yes, vegetarians, I know you can grill vegetables, too. Not my point. Calm down.)*

It's just that you don't really get that connection to primitive times and feel a visceral bond with your food if you're slapping lamb patties from Trader Joe's on your Weber. You should have to kill a damned sheep and drag it to your back yard.

I don't embrace outdoor cooking for the same reason I don't churn my own butter or do the dishes in a wooden barrel – because I don't have to!

Romanticize your primitive ancestors all you want; I like to believe that my forebears wandered for centuries looking for somewhere to plug in a toaster oven.

Beyond the convenience, cooking inside the home offers a multitude of advantages for the modern family. For instance, you'll probably have fewer bugs crawling near or landing on your food (unless you happen to be renting this studio apartment I had in Chicago).

And the most amazing benefit to cooking inside? If it starts to rain, you can continue to cook! Again, unless you're in that apartment I mentioned.

There's also very little subtlety to cooking on a grill for most folks. It's usually some guy on his fifth beer saying things like "How pink do you want your burger?" or "Could someone go back inside and get the ketchup?" And occasionally there's "How long do you think we can leave the potato salad out?"

Here's how nuanced grilling is -- a website purporting to be a complete resource for grilling techniques addresses the all-important temperature issue thusly:

> "So how hot is hot? The rule is to hold your hand above the cooking grate and start counting (until you can't hold your hand there anymore)…five seconds for 'low,' four seconds for 'medium,' two seconds for 'high.'"

Grilling culture (which apparently is not an oxymoron) is still dominated by men, I suppose because men are usually more about tools than technique.

I've had more than one male friend rave about his new grill in terms usually reserved for a new girlfriend. Not too many men will call you into the kitchen and say, "Hey, Jim, check out my new five-speed blender —she's a beauty, isn't she?"

Having never bought a grill, I was curious how much people spend for the pleasures of cooking *alfresco*. A hundred bucks? Five hundred? It is just a glorified fire pit, right? Then I found this:

The Talos Outdoor Cooking Suite is an open-air professional kitchen. The hand-crafted stainless steel exterior houses a 42" grilling area, three 25,000 BTU cast burners, a 20,000 BTU searing station and griddle, a hardwood cutting board, rotisserie, sink and a warming drawer. It even has a bartending station.

Because when the guys are over at my place ("It's show tunes night, guys!") I need almost FOUR FEET of grilling space.

Oh, and you can't *really* cook without having at least enough BTUs to power a steam locomotive. *And* I can't count the number of friends who have left my place disappointed because I don't have a dedicated 'searing station.'

I love that it's described as a 'professional kitchen.' I'm almost sure that anyone who can afford this probably could put all of these features in their ACTUAL kitchen, eliminating the need to go outside at all. But maybe I just don't get it.

Incidentally, the above model retails at thirty-five *THOUSAND* dollars. You and your friends could fly to Argentina for dinner with that money. Or, buy a couple dozen cows and you've got steaks for years.

Or you could buy a decent car for thirty-five grand and just go to a drive-through. In fact, the only way spending that much on a grill makes sense is if it somehow also functioned *as* a car. Now *that* would be something to brag about.

Hot Dogs and Haggis

When I first heard about the 'sport' of competitive eating, I had two reactions:

1. It's a sport?
2. It's really a sport?

What began as a rural novelty at county fairs involving homemade pies has somehow become a sport, with a governing body, sanctioned events, and over *half a million dollars* in annual prize money.

Most people point to ESPN for the sudden validation of recreational gorging. In the mid-seventies, the network televised the annual *Nathan's Famous* hot dog eating contest from Coney Island for the first time, and strangely, people watched.

Putting aside why someone would *enter* the contest, I can't *imagine* watching it. If I'm watching traditional sports, at least a part of the appeal is imagining (or remembering) me *playing* the sport.

What I've seen of competitive eating has *never* made me think, "If only it could be me up there on a makeshift stage eating really fast."

And I don't ever remember stuffing my face as a youngster and thinking, "If only I could turn pro at this, it could my ticket out of this town."

Don't get me wrong – I'm no stranger to overeating...just watch me in Vegas at a buffet. But I do that once every ten years or so. I've never thought of 'going pro.'

Really, if we're going to have people compete at basic bodily functions, why isn't there a competitive *sleeping* championship? I've been in training for the opportunity for years. You could have local mattress stores sponsor matches.

By the way, it's not just hot dogs that these 'athletes' shove down their gullets. There are competitions for eating asparagus, baked beans, beef tongue, Buffalo wings, burritos, cabbage, catfish, chili, cow brain (?!), and donuts. That's just the first part of the alphabet! Proving that, if we put our minds to it, Americans can over-indulge in anything.

Most events are timed affairs, except for haggis-eating contests. In those, I imagine the first person willing to *eat* haggis is automatically declared the world-record holder for haggis-eating.

For the uninitiated, in Scotland, haggis is traditionally served with mashed potatoes and rutabagas. For centuries, this has allowed the Scots to ignore the fact that their national food is a mix of sheep heart, sheep liver and sheep lungs. And I'm sure the whisky helps.

The International Federation of Competitive Eating (which, sadly, is a real thing) oversees the big money events.

They also enforce the rules about, for example, vomiting, and right there, you lose me as a sports fan. If throwing up is actually mentioned in the ground rules of the sport, I'm pretty sure I don't want to watch it on a flat-panel hi-def screen.

Apparently, the competitors prefer to call themselves 'gurgitators,' which may be the least pleasant word any group of people has ever *chosen* to call itself. And they all have nicknames, so I guess in that sense, they're like athletes.

For example, there's Don 'Moses' Lerman, who was quoted in an interview as saying *"I'll stretch my stomach until it causes internal bleeding."* Who says there are no more inspiring stories in professional sports?

The biggest name on the circuit is Joey 'Jaws' Chestnut, who started competing in college, and now holds several world 'records.' He used to be ranked second in the world, but like with any sport, there was a scandal:

> *The former champion was stripped of his title and ranking by Major League Eating and the IFOCE for refusing to sign a contract which would have prevented him from competing in non-MLE sanctioned events. I swear I didn't make up any of this.*

Despite the fact that competitive eating doesn't really make sense to me, I wanted to interview Joey

Chestnut for this piece. Then I found out these guys all have agents, like real athletes! How exactly do you 'represent' someone who does this?

"Mr. Chestnut will not be participating in next month's Pork Rind Championship, as we are negotiating with a very popular seafood restaurant regarding their annual oyster contest."

It's just as well I couldn't connect with anyone in this scene, things would have gone downhill after my first question:

"Do you realize that you could have fed several villages for a month with the amount of food you've forced into your pie hole during your 'career'?

I want to laugh at all of this, but I don't know that this is the best time in our nation's history to *glorify pigging out*. I don't mean to be rude, but we, as a country, could stand to drop a few pounds.

I have to admit, though, that on some level, competitive eating is *classic* Americana. It combines the two most characteristic American traits – gluttony and competitiveness.

More importantly, as a rich country with lots of natural resources and a habit of messing around with other countries' affairs, it's probably good to keep things low profile. Competitive eating is the kind of activity that inspires the rest of the world to hate us just a little bit more.

I'm Sensing a Theme Here

I suppose, if I were to make a 'bucket list" of things I want to do before I check out, I would have to put *'make bucket list'* near the top.

It's not that I don't make lists–mix my OCD with a little weed, and making lists becomes a necessity if I want to, say, accomplish anything.

And it's not that there aren't dozens of things I want to experience. The problem with lists of the *bucket* variety is that I don't want the pressure.

If I make a grocery list and forget to pick up milk, I can go back to the store for milk. When I meet my Vaguely Defined And Essentially Metaphorical God, I'd rather not be confronted with an itemized list of Things I Meant To Do.

I thought of all this because I had a friend visiting who wanted to go to a theme restaurant, and I realized I had somehow avoided that experience my entire life. And I intend to keep avoiding it.

I always imagined the 'experience' at a theme restaurant to be a combination of overpriced food and bad theater, neither of which make me want to leave the house.

Here in the U.S., the most successful 'concept' is probably Medieval Times, or as it's also known, "Where Kids Who Used To Play Dungeons And Dragons Work To Save Up Money To Go To Renaissance Festivals.'

"SORRY FOLKS. IN THE INTEREST OF HISTORICAL ACCURACY,
THE RESTAURANT IS CLOSED DUE TO PLAGUE

We also have Old West themed restaurants, pirate themes, 1920's gangster themes...all of which I *want* to mock, but on the other hand, ordering from a college kid in a cheesy wench costume may be as close to studying history as most Americans ever get. We like our education to come with an appetizer.

It's tragic how far we have fallen behind other nations in the bizarre-restaurant race. Beirut, Lebanon has a joint called 'Buns and Guns' that serves pizzas named after landmines (imagine the excitement when they announce "Claymore at table 5") and a sandwich called the AK-47. Ah, the wacky Lebanese.

In Nanning, China there's a place where the servers wear Mao-era Red Guard uniforms–I'm guessing they have a pretty strict 'no substitutions' policy there.

But no country can out-theme Japan. First time in Tokyo and want some local flavor? Bring the whole family to Nyotaimori, where you can eat sushi off a replica of a woman's naked body made of dough!

Or, maybe you're in Taipei–take your sweetheart to Modern Toilet, where, apparently, you sit on toilets while you eat out of toilets. And don't forget to check out the *several* cafes with a French Maid / Giggling Concubine 'theme.'

Look, my Japanese friends. You can stop pushing the envelope, weirdness-wise. We get it. You're smarter than we are, and much more clever. And you kick our ass when it comes to kitsch.

From Hello Kitty! to bubblegum pop music, Japan's win the game of Ironic Embrace. Now stop it. We get that having that many smart, intensely driven people on a tiny island can drive you a little crazy, but you *must stop* opening restaurants *based* on the crazy.

Besides, having your servers dress as mildly pornographic archetypes isn't exactly groundbreaking. We're the culture responsible for Hooters – we get it. And skimpy costumes do not, in a technical sense, make it a <u>theme</u>.

Unless you're saying the 'theme' is "Philandering Businessmen," in which case you should throw in some other characters. Have the hostess play a disgruntled 'wife,' and hire children to unexpectedly show up asking in broken English, "Are you my daddy?"

Which leads me to a few of *my* ideas for theme restaurants. Admittedly, I haven't fully fleshed out these ideas, and granted, I don't even have the capital to *eat* at most restaurants, let alone own one.

But if there are any bored venture capitalists out there reading this, here are some chances to get in on the next big thing . . .

 Like regional cuisine? Come to *Club DMZ*, a North Korean-styled eatery, where you'll dine on rice. Just rice. Call ahead to make sure they're not out of rice.

While waiting in an orderly line for your rice, take the opportunity to pledge loyalty to The Great Leader Who Makes Rice Possible.

Make sure to plan to arrive in time for the daily parade, when the entire wait staff combines with the kitchen staff for choreographed mass gymnastics displays.

 Your dining experience seems to never end at *Quagmire*, an authentic Afghani bistro.

Place your order, then watch in amazement as competing factions in the kitchen battle for control over your meal!

And tell Grandpa to bring his reading glasses, because the menu is in *twenty* different languages!

Feeling blue? Nurture your depression at *Wallow*. Miserable, hung over servers begrudgingly will wait on you and your friends, while the state-of-the-art sound system plays Nick Drake and My Chemical Romance.

 During their nightly Crappy Hour, all the drink specials are named after celebrity suicides– "Another round of Sylvias?" The lighting in the dining room is an exact recreation of a Norwegian winter.

Conservatives will be lined up around the block to get into the *Grand Old Pub*, the only restaurant dedicated to traditional American family values.

You may have to be patient waiting for your meal, as the Republican Party's anti-gay stance and removal of undocumented workers has left the restaurant woefully under-staffed.

History buffs will shout "Huzzah!" at the grand opening of *The K Man*, a restaurant devoted to the legacy of our eleventh president, James K. Polk.

Gleefully relive the years 1845-1849, and explore waistline expansionism as you try their signature omelette, the 'Manifest Destiny,' featuring a side of Texas Toast.

At (Law and) Order Up!, you'll be greeted by a pair of servers -- one a sarcastic, jaded veteran and the other a headstrong rookie who won't play by the rules.

Both of them will come back about twenty minutes after you order to "verify a few details and ask you a few questions."

A Word From Our Sponsor

Most food advertising seems pointless to me. I don't think I've ever watched an ad and then felt compelled to amend the grocery list for that week. Like most of us, in my foraging, I look for what's on sale.

That's why I think the only food ads on tv should be for places that deliver. Otherwise, we can all figure out what foods to buy on our own. Why advertise something like mayonnaise when anybody who wants mayonnaise can probably find mayonnaise *when they go to the store.*

And I don't imagine many people are swayed by an ad to switch *brands* of mayo just because of an ad – "Hey, darling – did you notice this other brand when you were at the market? Why the hell are we eating Best Foods? Why didn't you tell me there were other options?"

The first food ads were no doubt cave drawings that probably used the same approach we see today:

OG KILL EXTRA BIG BEAR. MANY PIECES AVAILABLE.

WILL PUT ON FIRE FOR YOU. ACT NOW.

IF GLOWING ORB IN SKY THREE TIMES, MEAT GONE.

Later, in the Middle Ages, you might have seen hand written flyers saying things like "Get thine mutton here! Our mutton has beene worm-free for a fortnight!"

Even as recently as the past century, food advertising was at least honest, by virtue of its simplicity:

It tells you where to get it, how much of it you get, and how much it costs.

The main difference in ads *today* is the emphasis on what isn't in the package -- "No Transfats!" "Zero cholesterol!" "Fifty percent less enzyme-modified hyperpolyunsaturated thiamine mononitrate than other brands!" I just think that, in the past, there was a little more emphasis on what *was* inside the box.

The worst part of most food ads is the slogan, a particularly insidious species of earworm that can stick to your brain worse than the hook from a Hall and Oates song.

So many of these are stuck in my mind that I can't walk through the grocery store without one of them bubbling up from the depths (incidentally, the Bubble-Up slogan was "A Kiss of Lemon, A Kiss of Lime." Seriously, I wish I didn't know these things).

The understated slogans work best for me, like Campbell's "Soup is good food." That's perfect! No made-up words, no miraculous claims, no CGI. What is it? Food. Is it good? Yeah. It's safe to say that soup is, in a general sense, good food. And that's all I need to know.

Or the classic, yet informative Velveeta slogan: "Colby, Swiss and Cheddar, blended all together." Of course, listing ingredients doesn't work for a lot of processed foods, because it's hard to come up with clever rhymes for 'pyridoxene hydrochloride.'

If you have a good product, you should be able to come up with a catchy slogan pretty easily. Instead, I'd like to be the guy who comes up with slogans for the kinds of foods I've had to buy when I've been broke.

"It's Exactly What You'd Expect For A Dollar!"

"It Sure Looks Like Salmon!"

"Better Than Not Eating At All!"

I hope that someday I get the chance to be a spokesman for something cooking-related.

"How many times have you been baffled by food-processors that have just too many functions? That's why I'm proud to endorse the KitchenAid One-Button Mixer.

No manual to read, no dials or attachments to decipher, just one big button! The patented 'blade' cuts vegetables really small, for all the times I need really small pieces of vegetables!"

I've also decided that for the next thing I write, I want sponsors. Why shouldn't writers be like NASCAR drivers? Most writers could use the money! We could wear patches on our blazers with sponsors' logos!

I'm gonna sell ad space right there in my book. If Frito-Lay wants to underwrite my next book with a few half-page ads for Ruffles, why not?

Or better yet, Nutella. They could even pay me in jars of Nutella.

Who am I kidding? For the right amount of money, I'd wear a giant hazelnut costume and sing their slogan. Which, if you're curious, is "Che mondo sarebbe senza *Nutella?*," or "What would the world be without Nutella?" What, indeed?

A Splendid Conversation

Sometimes I wonder, with the number of people *writing* about food these days, if anyone just *eats* food anymore. You might think that trying to appreciate food by reading about it is like trying to appreciate Mozart by looking at a *painting* of an orchestra.

Of course, at least if you're *reading* about food, you get the occasional picture to help you connect with the subject. But what could you possibly get from just listening to someone *talk* about food on the radio?

Turns out, a lot. 'The Splendid Table' is a weekly show on public radio, but you probably could have guessed the 'public part,' since I don't think the word 'splendid' gets used very often on commercial radio.

And calm down, right-wingers—I know you started salivating when you saw the words 'public radio,' but there's no scary liberal agenda here.

The host of 'The Splendid Table' is Lynne Rosetto Kasper, author of an award winning book on Northern Italian cooking called, oddly enough, 'The Splendid Table.'

Her show mixes interviews with food questions from listeners. They call it '"radio for people who love to eat." I call it...comfort radio.

When I set up our chat, I had two fears. The first was that somehow she would know that, though I've listened to public radio for years . . . I've never been a 'paid member.'

I've been *stealing* great music and conversation! I've been enjoying insightful political analysis *and* Tibetan throat singing without paying for either!

So I was afraid we might get to a really interesting part of the interview, and then someone from my local station would *interrupt* the phone call for twenty minutes asking me to make a pledge.

My second fear was that I would accidentally refer to her as Lynne RISOTTO Kasper, and then she'd get pissed, thinking I was mocking either *her* or the classic Italian creamy rice dish.

Thankfully, that didn't happen. She was very warm and down-to-earth, with none of the stuffiness you might think of when you hear 'public radio.'

I figured that she must get tired of answering questions, and I asked her whether she gets constantly bombarded with food questions wherever she goes. She was refreshingly honest:

> "I do, and quite frankly, I really don't mind it at all -- I rather like it. I have this job, on the radio . . . if people *weren't* interested, I'd be a bit surprised.
>
> It's fun to steer the conversation in other directions...but it's very flattering that people pay attention and have some idea what you do for a living."

She was understandably diplomatic when I wanted her to name a favorite guest *("It's hard to name names–it's like being asked to name your favorite restaurant")*, but she did single out quirky writer Amy Sedaris, saying *"she's just a hoot."*

The more *interesting* answer, I thought, if only for how *extraordinarily* carefully it was worded, came when I asked for her *least* favorite guest. Someone, let's say, whose *cooking* is more interesting than *they* are...

"I'm gonna put it this way . . . I'm not gonna name names -- *(Again with the not naming names? C'mon, lady, I'm trying to write a story here! I want to expose the dark side of public broadcasting!)*

There are *some* people that . . . lamentably do not . . . sparkle with life and do not generate . . . an immense amount of enthusiasm in others *(Got it–sort of the interview equivalent of powdered mashed potatoes).*

I found it encouraging that she admits to having been stumped --

"Oh, let me count the number of times! Oh my goodness, yes! Absolutely — I'm an expert at backpedalling. If you listen closely, a lot of what you're hearing is just logic, not 'knowledge.'"

"If you spend time involved in something you get a tremendous amount of pleasure doing, or being challenged by, you learn enough that, when people ask you questions, you can extrapolate."

I'll have to remember, next time I'm entirely guessing at something, to tell people that I'm just 'extrapolating.'

I thought it was time to make the questions a bit less ordinary, so I asked her: If a New York deli wanted to name a sandwich after her, what would you need to make the LRK?

"First of all, it would be made with a really, really chewy ciabatta bread.

It would be -- oh god, I haven't had this in ages -- really, really, REALLY good New York deli liverwurst . . .

With thin-sliced onion that has been marinated in a little vinegar to get rid of the heat of the onion."

"Those onions are shaved, they're piled on the sandwich, there's mayo on the bread, and mustard . . .

Now this is not a traditional liverwurst sandwich. This is MY liverwurst sandwich. This is the sandwich I ate growing up.

And you have this really chewy, fabulous bread — or, if you're on the east coast, you have a hard roll, which, unfortunately, nobody here knows what that is...It's cultural *(I hear ya. Nobody can make decent egg salad in Minnesota either)*.

The thing you *have* to have with that sandwich, and this is where deli traditionalists will raise their eyebrows and say 'She's a heathen,' is a great *sweet* gerkhin -- NOT a kosher pickle -- I know, 'she's a barbarian'..."

She's right. That *is* crazy talk.

But while she was on a roll (no doubt an east coast hard roll), I asked her to deal with a hypothetical dilemma:

Let's say I have to make a romantic dinner for someone, but I'm broke *and* I don't want to work too hard. Now . . . extrapolate!

"First thing you're gonna do is buy a potato . . . you're gonna buy an onion . . . and a carrot. And we're gonna get one can of tomatoes . . . and I'm gonna assume you have some herbs in the cupboard."

Initially, I thought she was asking if I had any *herb*, and then I thought of how cool it would be if Lynne Rosetto Kasper hosted "A Splendid Table" stoned. But back to my romantic dinner.

She asked if I had some wine around the house *(of course -- that's how I cope with being hypothetically broke)*, and whether I had any stale bread (what is this, 'Let's Make A Deal'?). Oh, and I would need some garlic and some oil or butter . . .

"You are gonna make her the best peasant soup in the whole world, and it's gonna warm her right to her toes.

You're gonna take a nice pot, put some butter in that pot. You're gonna slice up a lot of onion, and some of the carrots and put it in that pot, over medium to medium-low heat, and cover."

"Let it cook until the onions are soft, uncover it and let it brown. Stir occasionally, a little salt and pepper, if you have some allspice (or) dried basil *that* goes in...

Dice the potato and put it in, add some canned tomato to that, add some wine and enough water to cover just about everything. You're gonna let that simmer, and when everything's nice and soft, you can season it more . . .

Now what you're gonna do is a really classy Euro touch. You're gonna take your stale bread, heat it over a burner until it gets toasty.

You're gonna rub it with a little butter, and a half a clove of garlic. Break up pieces of that in the bottom of two soup bowls, and ladle that hot soup over it. *That* is a big bowl of love!"

I thought I could throw her a curve, and she nailed that one. But the questions only get more challenging . . .

See, she does this show from Minnesota, but she's also known for Tuscan cooking, so let's see if she can come up with a fusion of Northern Italy and Minnesota. What might be called . . . *Tuscanavian* cuisine. I suggested she use walleye:

"First of all, it's a fresh-water fish, so it's really, really simple. In most of Italy, fish is done SO simply. It might be done with a few sage leaves, in a pan, with olive oil or butter —in Minnesota, you'd probably use butter --

Anyway, you do a slow sauté of it, and literally just salt, pepper and maybe some slivers of garlic...You'd slow-cook it so you can be really careful of not overcooking, and you'd serve that with a few wedges of lemon and THAT IS IT."

Alright, she got that one, too. Unfazed and unrattled. There *had* to be a side of her that the listening audience never hears. I think deep down, we all want to imagine a cursing, angry Lynne Rosetto Kasper . . .

"Ohhhhhhhhhhhhhhh . . . there's a very colorful vocabulary that lurks just beneath the surface. There are things that aggravate me.

For instance that lovely pot of braising, slow-cooking loveliness? And you go to pull out the rack when the rack wasn't seated properly to begin with?"

"I love doing stock. I do it every three or four months. Make a big quantity, and stick it in the freezer. I've got this down to an art.

I leave it to sit overnight on the stove, very slow bubble. It's utterly delicious, it's like money in the bank, it's very easy to do.

Right now, I have a bad knee, so I'm in pain when I'm moving around the kitchen. So, I got this together, it was done, the pot was really heavy . . .

It was too big to fit in the fridge, and I wanted it cooled down really fast, and it was very cold outside, so I thought I'd put it on the back porch.

I was trying to get the screen door open, and I slipped with this pot, and the grease was still hot from the stove, and this stuff sloshed over the threshold, onto the cement steps . . .

Now there's freezing fat on the porch, you are ice-skating on this fat. it's midnight and I'm *chiseling* the porch . . . you have NO idea"

While I tried to get the image of this lovely woman ice-skating on chicken fat out of my head, I learned some random things about LRK as a chef:

Does she listen to music when she's cooking?

> "Generally it's just me and my food."

If she could only use one spice or herb for the rest of her life, what would it be?

> "The thing I turn to most often . . . it's a tossup between basil and some member of the chili family, leaning toward basil because it's a blending herb."

And about 'umami' ingredients like soy sauce and fish sauce that 'lift' other flavors, she says,

> "You keep those babies around the house and a little bit goes a long way to make food taste good."

She wouldn't say she hates any particular foods, but she did say, "Okra has yet to engage me."

She also mentioned that she no longer eats grains, and as much as she loves raw seafood, she avoids it

> "Because of problems I'm aware of. It's very disturbing that I have to, with what's happening to our food supply . . . Don't get me started. I know too much."

As intriguing as the phrase 'I know too much' is, I chose to move past the fact that apparently our entire food supply is full of 'disturbing' problems.

For a bonus question, I like to ask chefs where and when in history they would like to time-travel. Lynne gave me this answer, in the form of a history lesson:

> "I would like to be in the early 1500s, in the palace of the Dukes of Ferrara, in the Emilia-Romagna region of Northern Italy, during the height of their power.
>
> Lucretia Borgia had married into the family, and it was one of the great ruling houses of the Renaissance...
>
> To be the fly on the wall, to be both *at* those secret tables *and* observe what was going on in those kitchens. You would also be a first-hand observer of how poisons are prepared, all of the intrigue . . .

Of course, to understand someone who cooks, you need to know what their favorite utensil is:

> "It is my flat-bottomed wooden spatula, slightly curved at the bottom. Every time I see someone try to stir with a wooden spoon, it's like trying to move around food in a pot with the edge of a dime.

177

With my spatula you can sweep across the bottom of your pan quickly when something's threatening to burn...

I keep four or five of these at all times. When they look like they're gonna crack I get another one, because they're like...four bucks.

There are (two other) things that, without changing anything else you do, automatically make you a better cook. One is an oven thermometer. Every oven in the world is off. When you think you have failed -- 'I can't roast!' -- it's because your *oven* is messed up, not you!

And the other is, you get an instant-reading thermometer. That's gonna tell you, if your steak is really medium-rare, it's 130 degrees *before* you pull it off the heat to give it a rest...and you're always in control."

I wondered if our host had dealt with many 'stressed-out' callers in the midst of a culinary crisis:

"Early on when doing 'Turkey Confidential' *(her Thanksgiving advice show),* we had a young woman call in whose husband (they were newly married announced to his family that she was going to do Thanksgiving dinner all by herself, that she didn't need any help.

He was inviting his whole family over, and *she had never cooked.* My first thought was, ditch the guy. This poor woman called close to tears!

I really was thinking, I wish there were some way I could send this woman the name of a divorce lawyer.

So are there ever people who call the show, and it's clear from their questions they shouldn't even be **in** a kitchen -- that they should probably resign themselves to a life of ordering delivery?

Nowhere is it written that everybody is supposed to cook. I can roast something and know, by instinct, whether it's done, but can I figure out my computer? It's not my skill set!"

As we wrapped up the interview, Lynne offered some great insights about cooking as therapy, and about what matters most in the kitchen:

"When we're preoccupied with stress, or exhausted from work, to do something that occupies you physically . . .

Cooking involves *all* your senses, and if you can give yourself up to the *pleasure* of cooking, the goal doesn't have to be 'Did I get it right?' or 'Does it taste fabulous?'

That's very nice, but the real delight in this is that, for whatever amount of time you have, you can give yourself up to the taste, and the smell, and the touch.

To trust in your senses, and trust in your common sense. It's allowing yourself to become *totally* engaged in something that is *tactile*."

Which might be the best four-paragraph description I've ever heard of what cooking really *means*. Of course, she had me at 'big bowl of love.'

By the way, when I hung up the phone with Lynne, I made a donation to public radio. It wasn't a lot – every month I'll give about what you'd pay for an onion, a potato, a carrot, and a can of tomatoes. But now I can enjoy my Tibetan throat singing guilt-free.

Careful With That Blowfish!

Lately, I've started to *read* more about food than I have been, you know, eating it. I'm also discovering parts of the foodie 'scene' about which I had no clue. Like 'trending' foods.

I don't remember Mom ever serving dinner and saying, "Here you go, this is the latest food trend." I can't picture asking my neighborhood butcher which meats are 'trending' this year.

Frankly, I don't even like the word 'trending,' because usually I'm opposed to verbing nouns.

Apparently though, every year, a secret cabal of foodistas decide, for the uneducated communal palate, what foods will be hot in the next year.

Looking at lists from the past couple years, there seems to be no rhyme or reason behind what foods are 'trending.'

I looked at several lists from the past year, and then I got a little sad when I realized how many food trends I had missed.

Bean Soup

Having been poor during much of my life, I had always thought of bean soup as 'poor folks' food, but I guess being poor is trendier these days, so it makes sense. Of course, this means that next year we'll have to listen to hipsters whining about bean soup being *too* trendy.

Organic Chocolate

We're hip enough here in the hinterlands to be familiar with 'organic' chocolate, but I try to go one step further. I only eat free-range chocolate -- I don't want to imagine thousands of chocolate bunnies crowded into some windowless shed.

Canadian Cheeses

Why are Canadian cheeses on this list? Maybe they're not as pushy as your typical, swaggering American cheese — "Try this goat cheese from Ottawa. It's so well-mannered, not like those boorish American cheeses."

Organ Meats

I'm not denying that there are people who love their animal innards, but I'm not gonna buy that they're 'trending' until I see an 'offal aisle' at Trader Joe's. 'Organ meat' doesn't belong in the same sentence as 'trendy.' I'm still not sure it belongs in the same sentence as 'food.'

Whoopie Pies

All I know about whoopee pies is that they're Southern. Even Wikipedia is confused, calling them "an American baked good that may be considered either a cookie, pie, or cake." Also, I know that they weren't exactly 'trending' where *I* went to eat in 2010.

Bacon-Chocolate Chip Pancake Mix

There is a difference between 'trending' and 'a good idea I would try some time.' The only demographic group for whom this could be 'trending' would be potheads.

Sometimes I think the foodie fraternity is just messing with us normal eaters. I imagine they hold a meeting, then decide on some bizarre animal to tout as the next hip thing in food.

Then they stand around the granite islands in their high-tech kitchens laughing at us for eating . . . otter tails. While they chow down on some mac and Velveeta.

If foodies *aren't* messing with us, explain the appeal of blowfish. This is a fish that, when prepared properly, "has the consistency of white tuna, but with a more delicate taste." Oh -- but when NOT prepared correctly, it will kill you.

Call me boring, but I think there are enough food items that definitely will **not** kill me, even *if* I screw up when I'm cooking them, that I don't feel a need to try something that *might* kill me if my technique is a little off.

Another trendy food (apparently) is 'black garlic,' and when I read about it, I needed to learn more, because I use garlic in almost everything -- clove upon clove of clovey goodness.

I went to a website for a company that sells the stuff, and there was a description of how 'black garlic' comes into being:

"Black Garlic, Inc. uses the finest garlic. Our direct relationship with farmers enables us to select the raw garlic that will produce the best black garlic. Most of the magic happens behind the closed doors of our patented machine."

Whoa, back up there! That first paragraph seems all 'connected to nature,' and then you throw us a curve. 'Our patented machine'? Why 'behind the closed doors?' Mind telling us *what* exactly happens to the garlic *inside* the machine?

You know who should look into this? The Garlic Council. There must be one–there's an American Egg Board, and a Milk Advisory Board (which is where I go for all my milk advice).

There are dozens of other shadowy organizations, each bombarding us with propaganda for their special food interests. It always seems sad to me when foods have to lobby for our attention—we get it, pork, you taste good.

Of course, the list for following year was entirely different (foods only 'trend' for a year, I guess), and included 'tiny pies.' Please, for the love of Julia, explain to me why we need smaller pies, and why these freakishly small pies will suddenly become popular!

Are plate manufacturers scaling way back, or did the Pie Council poll a bunch of people who said "I like pies just fine, and I'd eat more of them, but they're always so big!"

One food item that is supposed to be hot this year is, coincidentally, another example of the convergence of the foodie and stoner mindsets.

They're called 'cakeballs,' and they are balls of cake...filled with ice cream. We're talking dessert squared here. They may not be trending nationwide, but I'm sure they're HUGELY popular with some twenty-somethings I know.

Ultimately, I think 'food trends' are a load of crap. I think they're just PR campaigns. Maybe the ostrich egg market takes a dive, and all of a sudden ostrich eggs are on the cover of *Gourmet* and everyone's buying gigantic skillets.

You know what food I think will be popular next year? Pizza. You know why? Because pizza will always be popular. Sure, there may be years when thick crust is in, or some odd combination of toppings, but the basic template of dough, sauce and cheese can't be beat.

Here's how perfect pizza is, conceptually—if your slice is topped with something you don't like, you just take it off and you **still** have dough, sauce and cheese! It's genius!

185

I recently did a comprehensive survey of more than five friends, and the results were interesting— when asked their favorite food, *nearly sixty-seven percent* chose pizza.

Granted, one person specified 'a thin crust pizza with Roma tomato sauce and mozzarella, topped halfway through with prosciutto and arugula until the arugula just slightly wilts,' but I got the impression that if it were a death row/last request scenario, he'd be fine with a plain slice of cheese from Domino's.

When it came to 'least favorite food,' there was more of a range of replies—beef liver, chicken liver (yeah, organ meats are really taking the country by storm), sardines, horseradish, and for some reason, somebody said 'creamed rutabagas.'

My question isn't "What was so bad about creamed rutabagas," but "Why would you even *try* creamed rutabagas?" Sounds like the Rutabaga Council was just getting desperate—"Look, nobody's buying these—maybe we should tell people to cream them, so they seem less like...rutabagas."

Modern, Schmodern

Unlike your typical fifty-something, I'd go so far as to say, overall, I'm in *favor* of *progress*. I have plenty of tech toys and gadgets that allow me to do literally *dozens* of things I didn't know I needed to do.

And, I actually know how to use most of the devices I own–although I'm pretty sure my phone is smarter than I am.

I also believe that every technological advance comes with a downside. Which is why, sometimes, I prefer the old way of doing things.

The aforementioned telephone is a perfect example. Sure, now I can press three buttons and find the nearest dry cleaner, or Ecuadoran restaurant.

Still, the old-fashioned rotary phone had its advantages. Foremost among them: when you have a rotary phone, you're a helluva lot less likely to drunk-dial employers, or ex-girlfriends.

With an old phone, you might want to tell her off, but by the time you're through dialing the area code, you've had time to gain some perspective.

Which brings me to molecular gastronomy. If you're not in the loop, it's like cooking, minus the nostalgia and warm feelings.

See, the theory is that we shouldn't be locked into making food the way Grandma did, when we have all this technology now, and just try to tell me that Grandma wouldn't have used a centrifuge if she could have *("Goshdurnit! I'm fixin' to turn this pecan pie into an industrial-looking aerosol foam!)*.

Me, I like 'comfort food.' Those two words just go together, like *good* and *sex*, or Turner and Hooch.

On a certain level, shouldn't all food be *comforting*? Nobody wants to hear the waiter say, "...and our soup this evening will make you particularly uncomfortable."

I also appreciate creativity, but I think there's a limit to how 'challenging' I want dinner to be. Yet that's what molecular gastronomy is all about -- using chemistry and physics to create new and interesting meals.

If I understand it correctly, it's designed for rich New Yorkers to enjoy from an ironic distance. Think of 'molecular gastronomy' as the bastard love child of Marie Curie and Mario Batali.

It's perfect for people who feel, "I want to cook, but I was hoping there could be more exposure to dangerous chemicals, and lasers."

The bible of the movement is called '*Modernist Cuisine*,' and it comprises five volumes and 2,438 pages.

The set even has its own trailer you can watch online. But I still think six hundred dollars is a little pricey for a cookbook, unless it also, say, predicts the future. Six hundred bucks is two months of *food* for us.

'Modernist Cuisine' has a dessert recipe for something called 'Garnet Yam Fondant with Sage Foam.' Since I'm sure the name alone has your mouth watering, let me parse the recipe for you.

If you want to liven up your next pool party with this treat, you'll need plenty of xanthan gum, isomalt and something called Versawhip; you'll also want a vacuum sealer, three pipettes, and a mandolin.

There's one step you're supposed to do for exactly 15 seconds, and something or other is supposed to be cut into 3cm by 1 1/4" tubes. Then you blanch the yam disks! Yum!

I swear, with all the references to emulsions and infusions in modernist cuisine, I'm not sure if they're making food or shampoo. Maybe 'sage foam' can be both. I don't know.

I'm pretty sure that for the last, maybe, all of recorded history, people have done just fine cooking with pots, pans and spatulas.

Not to mention that nobody has ever had a meal in a restaurant and told their waiter,

> "I'll have the special, but could you immerse it in liquid nitrogen? I'd like to feel like I'm dining in a laboratory."

The equipment alone for a 'modernist' kitchen is a little intimidating. Unless you scored a 4 or a 5 on your Advanced Placement science exams, do you really need to be using a 'rotary evaporator?'

How about a 'vitoceramicgriddle'? Let alone a twelve-hundred dollar 'immersion circulator.' I'd be too worried about meeting OSHA workplace standards, and waiting for an environmental impact study.

By comparison, let's look at the 'Country Kitchen Cook Book.' Published originally in 1911 by the *Dakota Farmer'* newspaper, this handy volume weighs in at a lean 150 pages.

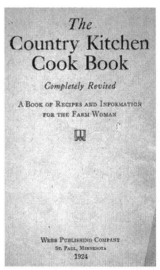

I have the 1924 edition, and you'll notice it's "Completely Revised."

You wouldn't want guests digging into some 'Stewed Prairie Chicken' and thinking, "Seriously? That is so 1911.

Most of the 'information' in here was common knowledge to the pre-Depression 'Farm Woman.' Seriously, who *didn't* know how to make 'Chicken Maryland,' or 'Broiled Squab on Toast Points ("Squab again, Mommy?")?

What makes this book a treasure are the various clippings that a woman named Mae kept tucked between the pages of the book.

Because of Mae, I now know how to make my own floor wax and furniture polish; and I also have hand-written instructions for making cheese biscuits

There's actually a recipe for making crackers. Shows you how spoiled by modernity I am -- I didn't know you *could* make crackers. I thought all the crackers on Earth were made centuries ago and boxed up by monks.

Autumn Dish Recipe Wins In Contest

Mrs. C. L. Thomas of Aberdeen has just been awarded a Certificate of Recipe Endorsement by Better Homes & Gardens for her recipe "Autumn Dish."

This certificate, which brings national recognition to Mrs. Thomas is given by Better Homes & Gardens only to distinguished recipes which pass its Tasting-Test Kitchen's high standards, for dependability, excellence of taste, and family usefulness

In addition to the signed certificate Mrs. Thomas also received six copies of her endorsed recipe, each bearing the Better Homes & Gardens Stamp of Recipe Endorsement, which she is giving to friends.

In awarding these certificates, it is the magazine's aim to provide proper recognition for the creative work done by women in their own kitchens, and also to raise the standard of accuracy and dependability of recipes as a whole.

Mrs. Thomas' endorsed recipe follows:
1 tablespoon butter
1 large onion, sliced
1 pint diced cooked potatoes
1-2 lb pork sausage
1 cup whole kernel corn
Salt and curry powder to taste
Milk.

Heat the butter in a skillet. Add the onion and fry until soft and yellow. Add the diced potatoes and brown slightly before adding the cooked sausage which has been broken into small pieces. Add the corn and season well with salt and curry powder. Add enough milk to moisten well. Simmer over low heat.

She saved a news item with the headline "Autumn Dish Recipe Wins In Contest," and as you read about 'Mrs. Thomas' and her 'Better Homes and Gardens Recipe Endorsement', you can almost picture Mae ripping it out in disgust and vowing to win in 1925.

By the way, the other side of this is a recipe for rabbit pie, taken from a booklet called "How to Dress, Ship, and Cook Wild Game," published by the *Remington Arms Company*! It's really too bad that *weapon manufacturers* got out of the cookbook industry.

I pass this one along, in memory of Mae, and all the other Farm Women who didn't need a digitally calibrated thermometer to tell when something was done. My favorite discovery in this book was stuck between pages 77 and 78, and it's Mae's personal recipe for 'Apple Crisp.' It's exactly what a recipe *should* look like.

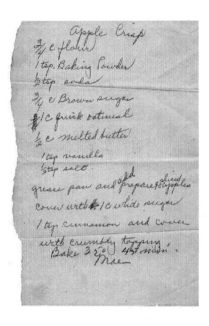

You can tell that Mae was experimenting every bit as much as today's hot shot chefs. Did you notice she changed the amount of oatmeal at the last minute? Brilliant, and no doubt based on years of empirical evidence.

I just wish Mae had told us what makes up the 'crumbly topping,' but that secret may have, sadly, died with her. Whatever it was, I'm almost sure you didn't need protective goggles or hazmat gloves.

Who Needs Recipes?

I think one of the few 'typically male' pieces of my personality is my unwillingness to read the instructions. To anything.

If everything is in the box that should be there, I should be able to assemble it or program it or hook it up without reading a freaking manual. I've assembled, programmed, and hooked up other things, how hard could it be?

I have a hunch that if I ever used a GPS device, I would end up arguing with the recorded voice that was giving me directions, or just get passive aggressive.

> "Fine. I'll turn left at Oak Street. You're probably right. What do *I* know; I'm just a human being, not some magical dashboard device. But you should know that *when* I turn, I will *not* be happy about it."

I'm the same way with microwave dinner instructions. The box may 'suggest' that, after four and a half minutes with the plastic covering 'vented', I remove the cover, stir the meal and then cook on medium for another minute and a half.

But instead, I'll just nuke the whole thing with the covering off for a total of 6 minutes *(I'm crazy, I tell ya!)*, because I'm hungry, and the entire meal cost two bucks!

The reality is, when I was younger, I probably went two or three years without eating anything that *wasn't* irradiated, so I'm willing to take some chances.

Given my aversion to instructions, it's probably no surprise that I substitute pretty liberally when I see a list of ingredients. The only time this is a bad idea is if you don't really know what a listed ingredient *is* (*I suppose I could use cinnamon instead of turmeric . . .*).

I've always had a problem with 'no substitutions' at restaurants, too. Now, I get that, at a steak joint, I can't substitute braised walleye for the top sirloin, but if you have what I'm asking for in the kitchen, and you cook said item on the *other days of the week*, you can make me a fish sandwich even if it's not the special for today!

The Girlfriend and I went to a restaurant a while back, and the 'vegetable of the day' was green beans. I'm sure all the veggies there were canned, but the day before, it was carrots, and I wanted carrots. My server told me: *"We can't do that."*

"So, you're telling me that, overnight, you guys *threw out* whatever carrots you didn't sell? Or is the guy who knows how to *heat up* the carrots *only available on Monday*?

I think what I lost at video poker should buy me a few carrots, don't you? OPEN A CAN OF CARROTS, YOU PUNCTILIOUS BASTARDS!"

I'm always substituting in the recipes I use. The earliest recipes would have had to be very simple. Probably cave drawings that showed an animal, a knife, and some fire. Not much room for creative substitution there.

The first *published* recipe book is believed to be the Latin collection called *"De re coquinaria,"* and attributed to Apicius, who was known as 'the Guy Fieri of ancient Rome."

I figured a Roman cookbook would just consist of the instructions "Take food from people you've conquered. Reheat." But there are some detailed recipes, for example, this lamb stew:

> "Put the pieces of meat into a pan. Finely chop an onion and coriander, pound pepper, 'lovage' *(leafy,* 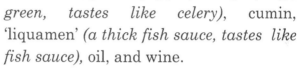 *green, tastes like celery),* cumin, 'liquamen' *(a thick fish sauce, tastes like fish sauce),* oil, and wine.
>
> Cook, turn out into a shallow pan, thicken with cornflour. You should add the contents of the mortar while the meat is still raw."

Sadly, my grocery story doesn't carry liquamen, or I would have given this a try. As willing as I am to substitute, everyone knows that there's nothing quite like liquamen. Ask for it by name!

I try to be careful with recipes I find online, because unfortunately, there isn't a National Internet Recipe Oversight Commission.

Sometimes the problem with a recipe isn't with the ingredients, but with the instructions. Especially if they're too precise, because then I feel like I'm just recreating that person's cooking success. It's like doing culinary karaoke.

I found a chicken recipe by someone named Joy Beeson, and although I'm sure she's a lovely woman, she seems a little . . . demanding in the kitchen. Check out these steps:

"Put half of a Knorr chicken-flavor bouillon cube into a #5 iron skillet. (8"/20cm dia.). Have ready another #5 skillet or an oven-proof lid."

Yeah, because I have *plenty* of '#5 skillets.' And does the *brand* of bouillon cube really matter?

"Add a generous crank of black pepper."

Oh, so you know the model number of the skillet but can't be more precise than a 'crank' of pepper?

"Add one tablespoon (1/16 cup) of cornstarch to the milk, cover tightly, shake vigorously, pour over the bouillon in the skillet. Heat to boiling point while stirring constantly, scraping the sides and bottom of the skillet with a spatula."

Well, after all that covering, shaking, pouring, heating, stirring (constantly!) and scraping, I've forgotten what I'm cooking.

"Do not dally between adding cornstarch and shaking, nor between shaking and pouring."

> So what you're telling me is, I can't dally at all. I suppose there's no lolligagging in your kitchen either.

"The cornstarch will settle out if it is given half a chance."

> Because all know how vindictive cornstarch can be.

"When the foam has settled to the bottom of the jar, pour that in with one hand while continuing to stir with the other. After five minutes, turn the thighs over, spoon gravy over them, cover tightly again, put skillet in oven. Immediately turn the oven to 200F."

> Okay, I'm not having fun anymore. This with one hand, that with the other, turning, spooning...and what if I want to wait a minute or two before turning the oven down? No—do it "immediately." Jeez.

"Ignore until serving time."

> The meal? The guests?

"One half hour before serving time, zap one large or two small potatoes and throw them naked onto the oven rack."

> For God's sake, don't dally if you're zapping! And this meal would be WAY more fun if you could throw the potatoes on the rack while *you're* 'naked.'

At one point, this book was going to be filled with recipes that express my unique vision as a cook, but based on feedback I got from publishers, I went in a different direction.

The rejection letters all droned on about the same supposed 'problems' with my recipes, namely:

Even though I'm not into the whole 'precision' thing with my cooking, I thought my recipes should be precise. I guess I went too far in the other direction when I specified things like *"Place casserole in 22.6 cubic-foot oven at 213 degrees Celsius for 47 minutes, 18 seconds."*

I thought it would be fun to have a section where the recipes all had blanks where temperatures and timings would normally be *("Bake for ＿＿ minutes at ＿＿ degrees. Now . . . can you solve the recipe?")*. I guess there was some fear of litigation with that one.

One last publisher's note might be helpful to anyone thinking of writing their own cookbook. Apparently they don't like you to use too many endangered species in your recipes. Too bad. My 'spotted owl stuffed with snail darter is quite good.

To be honest, I guess I'm just not a recipe kinda guy. Too confining -- stifles my creativity, and the joy of discovery, and blah blah blah. Sure, I'll *borrow* some ideas here and there, but if you ever have dinner at my place, you can be certain that some element of the meal will be a direct result of improvisation. And guessing.

The Pot Pie Pizza Process

In physics, fusion is the process by which two or more atomic nuclei join together to form a single heavier nucleus. Or, it's how you turn lead into gold. I can't remember. In music, 'fusion' refers to a blending of styles, like the jazz-rock fusion of Pat Metheny, or the jazz-crap fusion of Kenny G. 'Fusion,'

Not really sure what my point was. but 'fusion' is also used to describe food. Tex-Mex. Afro-Cuban. Kosher-Asian. Sometimes, cultural cross-pollination works.

On the other hand, I had to give up my dream of opening a chain of British-Korean restaurants ("*Kimchee-dilly Square*") when our market research showed that people didn't really want bland food that smelled bad.

My first fusion dish, like most of my truly inspired creations, came about because I was out of something. Here's the backstory:

The Girlfriend wanted pizza. I had, unfortunately, eaten the last slice of pizza. We also had no pizza sauce, and not much in the way of potential pizza toppings.

What we *had*, was a box of frozen na'an that I think had been in the freezer since 'Slumdog Millionaire' came out. Then it occurred to me – our na'an was already cut into pizza-slice shaped pieces!

Once again it was all coming together --ingenuity, inspiration, the ability to recognize simple shapes . . . and I would make *Na'an Pizza!* Or I could call it 'Non-Pizza!'

So I had a box of na'an, which sounds like the name of an alien on "Star Trek" -- "*I am Box of Na'an -- fear me!*" We had lots of fresh veggies, and some chicken breast from the previous night's feast, along with some homemade gravy.

I'm all set to assemble my Chicken Non-Pizza when I remember I have no sauce. I could *make* a sauce, but I had no tomatoes. No *stewed* tomatoes, no *diced* tomatoes -- not even a tiny can of tomato paste.

Here's where it gets a little weird. To recap, I had chicken, vegetables, and the aforementioned gravy. That's a pot pie waiting to happen!

But realistically, I wasn't going to take the time to bake a pie. The Girlfriend was hungry, and she wanted pizza. So, I made Open-Faced Pot-Pie Pizza. It's all the comfort of a pot pie, but easier to carry around with you!

Ingredients

- 3 pieces of frozen na'an
- Some leftover chicken
- Some leftover chicken gravy
- Some celery
- Some carrots
- Some mushrooms
- A piece of cheese

Instructions

Defrost the na'an. Meanwhile, chop the chicken, celery, carrots and mushrooms into pizza-topping sized chunks.

Take the na'an out of the oven. Carefully pour chicken gravy on each slice.

Place chunks of chicken, celery, carrots and mushrooms randomly on each slice.

Put a piece of cheese on one of the slices for The Girlfriend.

Put it all back in the oven for a while until it looks like pizza.

There you have it. An Indian-Italian classic. I'll admit I was worried about this one. I didn't want my mashup to be the food equivalent of those horrible 'crossover episodes' on TV. You know, where the cast of *'Beverly Hillbillies'* inexplicably visits *'Petticoat Junction?*

As it turned out, my mix of Milan, Mumbai, and the Midwest was a hit. I'm already thinking about what I'll combine next.

Maybe I'll put German sausage on a French baguette and call it a Vichy Sandwich. Or I might mix Newfoundland and New Orleans, and create . . . whatever that would be. All I know for sure is that, through my cooking, I am single-handedly bringing the world together, one dish at a time.

Note: I have since withdrawn my trademark application for the name 'Pot Pie Pizza,' as there are, according to the web, "about 168,000" people who have used that phrase.

There are also at least 77,100 people who have invented "naan pizza," and 65,800 who beat me to the phrase "non-pizza." Damn you, Google.

What Do You Call *That*?

I'm never sure how to describe what it is I write. I could say, "I write short humorous essays, sort of like how newspaper columns were, but in first person, like a blog," but that's not very catchy. It's not exactly 'high concept.'

I could combine the two concepts and tell people I write 'blogumns.' Sure, it's a little Tolkeinesque, but haven't you always thought there should be more words in English that end in 'mn?'

What you call something matters. Take rock and roll. I think even die-hard fans of 'My Backyard' and 'The Polka Tulk Blues Band' would have to admit that Lynyrd Skynyrd and Black Sabbath are better band names.

It's the same with food. There are certain foods that I'm convinced wouldn't sell at all if they had different names. Or more accurate names.

If you've ever had *beignets*, you know they're a delicious filled pastry popular in New Orleans. But I'm guessing the lines at Mardi Gras would be a bit shorter if they were called "Deep-Fried Dough Balls (which *should* be a band name)."

Sometimes all it takes is a vaguely evocative name to distract people into buying an otherwise odious food. Case in point: 'Vienna Franks."

These little Franken-franks are composed of a disturbing paste made from chicken and pork and beef and turkey . . . parts.

Then the 'franks' are stuffed in a can in some sort of briny sauce. Since they're Viennese, though, people think they're being cosmopolitan.

Anyway, even though I KNOW they're already *cooked*, they always look to me like they need to be cooked *again*. That seems wrong.

Leave it to the gastronomically-challenged Brits to come up with a questionable food *idea,* and then give it a name that sounds even more abhorrent. It's bad enough you serve steamed suet pudding–for God's sake, do you have to call it 'Spotted Dick?"

Call me square, but I like the *name* of a dish to give me *some* indication of what might be *in* the dish before I *order* the dish.

Recently voted the best restaurant in the world, *Noma* in Copenhagen has an entrée called 'Oyster and the Ocean,' and that is a bullshit name.

Again, I'd like to know exactly what comes *with* that oyster and what you've done with it. Not just where you got it. Same reason I wouldn't order something called "Chicken and Stuff From The Ground."

I dig those long, enigmatic, conceptual names you see on menus in Chinese restaurants. "Ants Climbing A Tree" may not sound as *appetizing* as 'marinated ground meat over noodles,' but at the same time, I kinda *like* having my dinner tell me a little story.

One night I ordered something called "Bean Curd Made By A Pockmarked Woman," which is such a great name it should count as dinner *and* a movie.

I never know what to call the things I cook, but I feel I have to call a dish *something*. It always seemed lazy to me for an artist to call a painting 'Untitled."

 This was done by the Australian Charles Green Shaw. Here's an idea, Chuck. When you're *done* with your painting, take the extra five minutes and tell me what it's supposed to be. It doesn't have to be literal, but at least make an effort.

When I do try to name a dish, in case I want to recreate it, I'm usually *too* literal. That's because I figure, if the name of the dish contains enough details, I'll remember how I made it.

Unfortunately, The Girlfriend has yet to ask for my 'Tortilla Crusted Spinach Topped Curried Chicken Thighs,' so I'm thinking I need punchier names.

Sometimes I try to be too clever. We had small burgers on English muffins a while back, which I now insist on calling 'Royal Sliders.' And the cheap cut of pork I braised in beer – I call that dish "My Drunk Butt."

There are times when I come up with a great name for a dish *first*, and then I figure out what might go in it. I have yet to make creation called 'Peaches and Herb Chicken,' but if I ever go to a seventies party, that's what I'm bringing.

I never come up with good names for my ground turkey entrées, because no matter what I might want to make out of pound of Jennie-O, it always ends up as meatloaf.

It reminds me of when my mom crocheted. Despite telling me every year that she was making me a sweater, it always turned into an afghan on the back of our couch.

Once, I got ambitious and made a turkey *roll*, and it looked perfect. I put it in the oven, and when I took it out, it had settled and flattened and . . . become yet another meatloaf.

I decided if I were going to keep making variations on meatloaf, I would need to be more creative with the presentation. Hopefully that would inspire a more creative name.

The next time I made a meatloaf, I made it *in a square casserole pan,* the kind in which you would bake a cake. Right there, it would be different than its boring loaf cousins, because, hey, it's now a meat *cake.*

When it was done, I sliced it in half *sideways*, and spread a thin layer of *mashed potatoes* on the bottom layer. I know – I was out of control!

But that wasn't the end of my innovation. I replaced the top half, and topped the whole thing with two kinds of crumbled up crackers!

I call it "Double Crumb Comfort Cake." It's catchy, it's fun to say, plus it's got a built-in slogan for marketing –

"Sounds like dessert, but tastes like dinner!"

I Need a Catchphrase

There's always a little down time when you're cooking, whether you're waiting for your eggs to poach, your onions to get translucent, or your roux to . . . get roux-ey enough.

I think cooking is like baseball, or jazz, in that, to enjoy them, you have to get past the fact that, in all three, there seem to be times when nothing's really, you know, *happening*.

The biggest difference between the three is that Ken Burns hasn't done a twelve part documentary about cooking. Yet.

I use my idle time in the kitchen thinking about philosophy and coming up with crackpot theories, which I suppose should be called *crockpot* theories.

I don't bother with meaning-of-life stuff, since that ground has been covered pretty well. I like to *fold* my philosophy *into* my cooking, like I'm making a piecrust out of ideas. And pie crusts should be flaky, right?

I wrestle with the questions that have troubled cooks for centuries, like "Can you cook chicken in beef stock?" Which, by the way I will not do. It just seems wrong and disturbing.

Or, "Is it wrong to have rice AND potatoes in the same meal?" This is known amongst philosopher-cooks as the Starch Conundrum.

As much time as I've spent *thinking* about cooking, I have yet to figure out the answer to the fundamental question all aspiring chefs should ask themselves—"What is my catchphrase?"

A cook without a catchphrase is just...someone cooking! Who would want to watch that?

From "Kick it up a notch" to "Yummo," the chefs making the big tv bucks all have a phrase or a word that brands them.

It's the thing they say when they add the lemon zest, or make peaks in their meringues. I need one of those.

Initially, I wanted it to be just one syllable -- one big flavorful syllable, like Emeril's "Bam!" By the way, why does he get "Bam!" *and* ""Kick it up a notch"? I think he should have to pick one and give the other one to an up-and-coming chef.

At one point I thought I found my catchphrase when I spent a week or two saying "Boom!" while I was cooking. Now, I'm new at this, so I may have overused it.

I guess it's overkill to shout "Boom!" when you're just, say, adding a sprig of parsley. It didn't matter, because some sandwich guy on the Food Network beat me to it.

I considered going really retro with some vintage slang. I could shout "Applesauce!," but that really only makes sense if I've just made applesauce.

I really like 'pish-posh,' and it sorta *sounds* like a food item (*"I'll have the curried pish-posh"*), but it's a bit too snooty for the food I like to cook.

I desperately wanting something as my trademark exclamation, and I wanted it to have a little worldly cachet.

I went online and found a phrase I really liked -- "Ahnaal Natrakh," which was supposedly part of a Merlin's Charm of Making. That could work – it tells people, this guy is making some magic!

Unfortunately, after I'd rehearsed how I would use my new catchphrase, I learned that "Ahnaal Natrakh" is also the name of a death-metal band in the UK, known for songs such as "Castigation and Betrayal" and "Screaming of the Unborn" off their album "Hell Is Empty and All The Devils Are Here." That wasn't really the vibe I'm going for.

I could turn to pop culture, but all I could think of were sci-fi catchphrases like "Resistance is futile!," which would be dramatic but maybe overly pushy *("And now, you garnish the soup, and admit that RESISTANCE IS FUTILE!")*.

What about something more old school. Every time I add an ingredient I could say, "By the power of Greystoke!"

Superheroes always have catchphrases, so I could go that direction, but then I'd have to wear a cape and a tights when I cook (*there's* a mental picture for you).

The Torch's "Flame On!" would work unless you're dealing with an electric range, in which case you would have to shout "Warm Up Gradually!," which doesn't really have the same impact.

Eventually I hit a wall and just started trying random phrases. How about *"Take the next train to Tastyville?"* I could go edgy with *"Put that in your Dutch oven!"* Or take the understated approach, my trademark phrase could be "Now THAT'S edible!"

In the end, I found my catchphrase by turning back to music and my cooking playlist.' In Nat 'King' Cole's 'Frim-Fram Sauce,' the singer lists the foods he *doesn*'t want, and ends each verse with the same gibberish words:

I want the frim-fram sauce with the ausen fay
With chafafah on the side.

Well, there's *three* potential catchphrases nobody's using. 'Ausen fay' isn't terribly catchy, but 'frim-fram is perfect, because it could refer to anything you throw into the dish. "Now let's add some frim-fram!"

But even better is *chafafah*. Not only does it sound like an exotic food (something you might have with a side of tabouli), it's just plain fun to say!

"Next you'll put in your basil and, **chafafah!**"
"Dredge the pork in the flour and, **chafafah!**"

The best thing about it is, since it's a made-up word, you can even use it as a curse word if you want:

"*I put in too much salt -- chafafah!*"

Go ahead and laugh, but by next year you'll be flipping through your Williams-Sonoma catalog and see a full line of CHAFAFAH™ kitchenware. Aprons, cutting boards, spatulas, you name it – I'll put my catchphrase on it.

Until Williams –Sonoma *decides* to carry these,
they're available at *my* website, MeatloafMuffins.com.

211

Cooking is Believing

Every so often you hear about someone who claims to see a supernatural being in their food. Jesus in a piece of toast, or the Virgin Mary in a stack of pancakes. For some reason, it's usually a breakfast food.

Although I've had some food come out looking a little odd, I've never seen any signs of God in my scrambled eggs. But sometimes, when every part of a meal comes together, and the presentation is just right, I believe in . . . something.

Bear in mind, my idea of God isn't very mainstream. I *can* say, unequivocally, that I believe there is *some sort* of vague, nebulous energy source that's involved *somehow* in the way the universe works. But an old bearded man smiting people? Probably not.

See me in the kitchen, though, and I become significantly more . . . connected to God.

I'm constantly either praying something won't be overcooked, or begging for divine intervention to thicken a sauce, or imploring the heavens to make my side dishes come out at the same time as the main course.

I figure, there may not be a 'god,' but on the off chance that there is, why not ask for a little help?

Sometimes, I envy the Hindus. Not so much for the finger cymbals, but for the polytheism.The way I see it, if you're gonna believe in what may well be a mythological being, why not believe in a whole gang of them? And on those rare occasions when I hit it out of the park when I'm cooking, it would be nice to be Hindu so I could have more gods to thank.

The Chinese have a dedicated Kitchen God, a fellow named *Zau Jun*. It literally means 'Stove God,' but I'm guessing he handles the *entire* kitchen. According to tradition, he returns to Heaven just before Chinese New Year to report on the activities of every household during the past year.

Then the Jade Emperor either rewards or punishes the family based on Zao Jun's annual report. And that's the problem I always have with gods. They're always so...judgy.

BY MY COMMAND, YOU SHALL HENCEFORTH COOK POULTRY TO AN INTERNAL TEMPERATURE OF AT LEAST 170 DEGREES

Roman Catholics don't have a *god* specifically assigned to kitchen duty, but they do have TWO patron saints looking out for cooks.

Saint Marta was the sister of Mary Magdalena, and she is said to have cooked meals for Jesus. Talk about a high-pressure catering gig! You *really* didn't want to mess up His appetizer order.

Then there's St. Lorenzo. Not only a patron saint of cooks, Lawrence is sometimes thought of as a patron of comedians.

That's because, when he was being martyred on a bed of burning coals, the legend says that he quipped, "Turn me over. This side is done." Which I suppose would also make him the patron saint of grilling.

My personal spirituality is pretty eclectic. To put it in a food context, I tell people I'm a Smorgasbordian. I sample a little bit from all the major faiths, but I try not to fill up on any particular one.

Some days I'm not all that hungry, but other times I might have a craving for Eastern mysticism, or maybe I'll go back for a second helping of Jewish angst.

If any culture *really* gets how important food is, it's Jewish culture. Forget all the ephemeral, heavenly symbolism and the learned scholarly debate about arcane theological points -- most Jewish gatherings are all about the here and now. And the food.

When I converted to Judaism as an adult, one of the first things I learned was a saying that explains every Jewish holiday:

"They tried to kill us. We survived. Let's eat."

I could never think of a way to connect my Judaism to my cooking. I wasn't raised Jewish, so I don't have nostalgic memories of making latkes standing next to my *Bubbe*.

Then I figured out a way to bring together my Jewish faith with my cooking style, by way of the Yiddish language. First of all, I had been using Yiddish words and phrases since well before I became 'officially' Jewish.

More importantly, it occurred to me that Yiddish is the perfect language for cooking. Maybe not everyone's cooking, but definitely mine.

My cooking is imprecise, and hard to define – just like Yiddish! Ask any two Jews what a Yiddish word means, and you're likely to get at least three different answers.

I got to thinking about how various Yiddish words and phrases might apply to certain kitchen situations, and then I realized I needed to call my rabbi.

 By 'my rabbi,' I mean the rabbi who taught my conversion class and then officiated while I recited Hebrew, floating naked in a ritual bath (*I* was the one floating and naked, *not* the rabbi).

Rabbi Alan Shavit-Lonstein at Temple of Aaron in St. Paul is a great teacher, and since we hadn't chatted in a while, I thought it would be fun to get a more learned take on Yiddish in the kitchen.

As he explained it, the strong connection I feel between Yiddish and my approach to cooking is something known in Hebrew as 'tam v'reach.'

Literally meaning *'taste and smell,'* 'tam v'reach refers to something that

> "captures the Yiddish spirit without having any Yiddish ingredients from history or culture . . . It's got the taste and smell of it, without . . . It's like kosher-style, like kosher dill pickles make it a Jewish event somehow . . . "

I wanted to have the rabbi define some Yiddish terms in a cooking context. For instance, could someone be *verklempt* over a meal?

> "Absolutely, and it can be both a positive ane a negative . . . you can be so moved, and awestruck, and blown away by a meal --you can be so thrilled by it . . .
>
> or so disappointed by it, or so overworked from having to prepare it and then nobody appreciates it. I think after every meal, a good Jewish response could be "I'm verklempt."

I asked him if there were a cooking scenario in which you might, conceivably, *plotz*. The rabbi's answer encapsulates, in concise form, thousands of years of Jewish logic and higher thought:

> "If you're a *plotzer*, I guess, then yes."

Despite what sitcoms would have you believe, *'schlemiel'* and *'schlamazel'* were around before 'Laverne and Shirley.' The rabbi shared a definition:

> "A *schlemiel* is someone who comes up with the stupidest idea ever, and the *schlamazel* is the one who thinks it's brilliant. (For example, if I were to suggest to The Girlfriend that we have lutefisk for dinner, and if she were to say that sounded great.)

My favorite Yiddishism, and one I learned from my rabbi, is the conjunctive adverb 'davka.' As befitting a Yiddish word, I found several definitions. Here are a couple from the Rabbi Alan:

> "Two definitions are useful . . . you can define it using that scene in 'Casablanca' where Bogart says *"Of all the gin joints in all the towns in all the world, she walks into mine."* So you put in *davka* there -- *davka* she walked into mine . . .

> It's that sense of *'Woe is me'* and *'Of course'* and that Jewish *'Here we go again,' and 'It's happening to us . . . I <u>had</u> to suffer this way.'*

> And then there's the piece of davka when someone will do something 'davka' it means they're doing it even though they know it's annoying, and probably because they *know* it's annoying they'll keep doing it."

"If you have an ingredient that you *davka* throw in because, you know, that's just the way you are. It doesn't make any sense, there's no reason for it, it doesn't fit the flavor profile. There can be 'davka' ingredients . . .

There are people that get on kicks -- they read somewhere that, say, ginger . . . cleanses their bodies. So *davka*, they have to put ginger in everything."

It's a deep word, 'davka.' I should probably only bring out that word if I'm cooking for a holiday seder or something like that. *Davka*, I intend to use it *all the time*.

We didn't get to all of the Yiddish words on my mental list, but trust me, they *all* apply to cooking and food somehow.

Unfortunately, we had to wrap things up because I was dealing with a lot of *tsouris*, and on top of that I had to *schlep* to the *facacta* store with a little *mazuma* because we had *bupkis* in the house to eat, and I get a little *meshuggah* if I don't have a *nosh* . . .

Oatmeal for Supper

I recently had a chance to talk with an inventive chef with forty years of kitchen experience -- a web-savvy culinary veteran known for an adventurous palate and resourcefulness under pressure.

She's as comfortable preparing *crème brûlée* as they are wild game. I'm referring, of course, to my friend Carl's mom.

Carl is extremely Scandinavian. One of four children of a mixed-marriage (father is Norwegian, Mom is, if you can believe it, *Danish*), he looks so Nordic I always expect him to be skiing while carrying a rifle.

Turns out, he's more Frisbee golf than biathlon, but he definitely *looks* like his heritage. He's from Willmar, Minnesota, doncha know....

Willmar is a town of about twenty thousand people almost exactly halfway between the equator and the North Pole. Machine Gun Kelly pulled off a notorious bank heist here in 1930. Big railroad town.

According to the town's website, it's "the fastest-growing non-metropolitan area in Minnesota" (just a tip, city planners–when choosing a slogan, shorter is usually better. Think in terms of 'City of . . . something').

Carl and I were talking about the book and he said I should talk to his mom. I thought, why not *interview* her? I figured I'd get a couple of cute homespun stories and a little local flavor. I ended up getting a cooking education.

It's weird interviewing someone's mom. I figured I would dial down the snark a bit; after all, this is someone's *mom*.

Also, what do I call her? Her name is Mary, but that feels way too familiar. I tend to treat moms the same way I would an ex-president. Whatever I might think of the *person*, I always respect the *office*. So I think I'll go with 'Mrs. Olson.'

For you children of the tube, I don't mean the 'Mrs. Olson' from Folger's
Our Mrs. Olson made it a point to tell me that Folger's is their "everyday coffee – not for company."

Mrs. Olson took time out from a vacation to give me a look into the world of an unheralded chef who has spent decades in the cooking trenches. And you want authentic? During our half-hour interview, she gave me two *"there ya go"*s, one *"oh my word"* and a *"you betcha."* So have a seat, get your elbows off the table, and pay attention to Mrs. Olson.

At least twice a month for forty years, Mrs. Olson has made some version of what we call 'hotdish' (state law requires any interview with a local chef to include a question about 'hotdish').

That's over a thousand freaking casseroles and at least a thousand cans of Campbell's Cream of Mushroom Soup, but when I asked her if the thought of all that made her tired, she just said, *"Noooo, it's part of motherhood."*

Do the math -- this woman has prepared at least two meals a day for almost half a century. Oh, and she's been doing it without a lot of gadgets.

She owns a food processor, but she bought it to make one specific thing (a British shortbread recipe) and that's *all* she uses it for. When I asked her what her favorite utensil would be, she thought for a few moments, and then said *"It would have to be my wire whisk."*

Mrs. Olson learned about cooking at a young age:

"My mother cooked absolutely fabulous…and (she was) a baker! I used to envy the kids that could have Wonder Bread—all our bread was homemade.

She was a fabulous cook. She was happy in the kitchen…she was ten when her dad died and there were nine children in the family, and she said she got stuck in the kitchen and learned to love it."

Carl's maternal grandma may have been a "fabulous cook," but to hear *him* tell it, she made one horribly memorable mistake.

Allegedly, one day she made beet jello. Now I'm with you. The words 'beet' and 'jello' should never be that close to each other.

I don't even want to hear someone say "I had some beets, and then later had some jello." There should be at least a paragraph between those two words at all times. But let's have mom address the incident:

> "She knew he liked beets, and she found a recipe for it—it wasn't beet <u>jello</u> it was beet <u>gelatin</u> *(that's much more appetizing)*.
>
> It was 'formed,' and to him it was jello. She was just so pleased when she brought this to the table, and then he couldn't eat it . . .
>
> In the spirit of full disclosure, I asked if she tasted it --
>
> No, no, no. It had chunks of cucumber, and diced celery . . . It's like she had cooked them and ground them up, almost like an aspic?
>
> And it just . . . ohhhhhhh. *(By the way, in print you can't tell, but it wasn't a good 'ohhhhhhh.')*

Before I talked with his mom, Carl told me that "she was at the vanguard in bringing ethnic cuisine to small-town Minnesota," and I *love* having friends that use the word 'vanguard.'

However, Mrs. Olson was quick to deflect any praise.

> "Noooooo, that was his take on it. But one of my favorite things to do is to walk through the grocery store, and if there's something I haven't seen before and I don't know what it is, then I look at the package for directions.
>
> If not, I buy it, bring it home, and go online. The internet is indispensable!" *I didn't have the heart to tell her that some things on the internet aren't true.*

In addition to her cosmopolitan (and seemingly random) approach to meal planning, she hasn't lost touch with her Scandinavian roots.

She mentioned römmegröt, which I've since learned is a porridge made from sour cream, whole milk, wheat flour, butter and salt. Apparently, you can add cinnamon to it to make it more like . . . food.

And not many people rave about *lefse*, a traditional Norwegian flatbread; that's probably because it's traditional, Norwegian, and flat.

Mrs. Olson was quick to defend lefse as anything but boring:

> "There's *nothing better* than soft, fresh right-out-of-the-pan lefse with butter and sugar. I make the dough, but the boys still do the rolling and baking. It's the kind of thing, when everyone's together right before Christmas . . . you like to keep people busy."

Speaking of family, I asked about her husband, and she told me

> "He wasn't around a lot. He had a very intensive, demanding job, so he would show up for meals and take off again."

Which makes me imagine that her husband was some sort of spy, working dangerous undercover missions under an assumed name, undercover in small-town Minnesota, but I have no proof of this.

Even without an espionage subplot, I figured with four kids, there had to have been *some* drama at mealtimes, so I asked her how she handled the inevitable 'finicky eater.'

> "I don't have a lot of patience with that. You know, you say grace, you bless the food...and you don't wanna eat it?"

And to the age-old problem of getting kids to eat their veggies, she suggested some tips:

> "You can put vegetables in places where they don't take 'em out so easily (*in the lefse dough?*). You can sneak 'em in places. And even the most finicky eater will eat them raw with a dip.
>
> I always figured they had to take three bites of something, and if they didn't like it, I didn't push it, because sometimes kids have a definite aversion to something."

I wish she would have been *my* mom -- I couldn't have gotten away with telling my mom I didn't want to eat something because I had an *aversion* to it.

Flipping the question around, I asked Mrs. Olson if there was anything *she* wouldn't eat. As an example I mentioned my antipathy toward beef liver, it seemed like I touched a nerve.

> "Yeah, I don't eat that anymore. We had to eat it once a week when I was growing up and . . . I will never eat that again."

As experienced in the kitchen as she might be, Mrs. Olson knows her limitations. She offered a lovely, pastoral story of Carl's brother, a fox, and a crockpot . . .

"One day he *did* shoot a fox and he skinned it and he says, 'Mom, you gotta cook this -- it was like skinning our dog!' He said 'I just hate to waste it.'

And so I called several of the older women whose husbands hunted and said, 'How do you cook a fox?' and one of them says, 'Mary, I've never heard of anybody cooking a fox. I don't know if it can be done.'

So, I put it in the crockpot, with lots of celery, and onions, and tomatoes, and it wasn't too long and the smell of wet fur filled the house.

I brought the fox out and I said to Mark, 'You take the first bite,' so he did, and he said 'Mom, why don't you just take it outside. Just . . . take it outside.'

Years later, I read *'A Year in Provence,'* and there's story of an old guy who would *tell* people how to cook fox -- and it was a joke! You *cannot* cook fox."

We went to happier memories when I asked her about a dinner for Carl's groomsmen. There were about forty people, and she prepared a whole *twenty-five pound* salmon.

Of course, with the salmon, she also prepared baked potatoes with rosemary, lemon, and balsamic vinegar, and a whole head of cauliflower that was on a bed of baby peas with a smoked gouda sauce, and two kinds of salad, and four kinds of pie. You know, like anyone would . . . anyway, back to the salmon:

> "I did *not* think ahead. I didn't have a pan for anything that big, so I had to construct a pan. I put two jelly roll pans together with layers of aluminum foil . . .
>
> It filled up the whole oven, so of course then the air couldn't circulate, and the salmon took *forever* . . . GAAAH! *So* embarrassing. But it tasted fine."

Like all great chefs, Mrs. Olson has needed to think on her feet. She shared with me an example of how she's turned cooking mistakes into innovations:

> "My favorite thing to make is a scratch thirteen egg-white angel food cake. Once, I took it out of the oven too soon, and you tip it over a bottle, and the whole thing just fell, all over the countertops.
>
> But I decided, well, there ya go! So, I scooped it in dishes with fresh raspberries, and it was something no one had ever had before."

Even the most seasoned chefs have their stories of dining debacles. For instance, here's a story with all the elements of classic horror: a birthday party, baking, and fifth-graders left to their own devices:

"My daughter was having a birthday party in fifth grade. So I thought, what I'd do with all these girls, is I'd put them in teams of two, and I put all the ingredients for a cake on the table, and they would have to put the cake together without a recipe . . .

Well, one of the girls got the garlic powder out. The whole house smelled very strange, and because there was no proper measuring of the leavening agent, the oven -- there were flames in the oven, smoke in the house . . . *that* was a wonderful disaster."

Her other personal 'kitchen nightmare' happened when she was a newlywed --

"Soon after we were married, we invited some of the relatives over, and I had never, as a single gal, put together a meal with various courses, and *nothing* was ready together. Some things were overcooked and some things weren't started, and it was *so* embarrassing."

Forty years, and those are your worst cooking disasters? None of *those* stories involve injuries, or things blowing up!

Later, she gave me some insight into one of the biggest reasons she makes things from scratch, *despite* the risk of mishap.

> "To keep it interesting. I used to make my own graham crackers, for example, and all kinds of fun things. You know, when you're home all day, and you have four kids in five years . . . you just give 'em each a bowl, and go to it! It's a mess, but it's two hours killed."

Even when talking about making a romantic meal for her husband, Mrs. Olson demonstrates old-fashioned heartland practicality and thrift. Phil's favorite dessert is *crème brûlée,* and I mentioned that I'd like to make it, but I don't have one of those blowtorch thingies —

> "I was at a kitchen shop, and they are *thirty-five dollars,* for the cheapest one I found! After (the crème brûlée) is chilled, I just put it under the broiler with sugar on it, and they all get done at the same time.
>
> You have to watch it, but that's the way they do it in France. (The torches are) just something more to sell at the kitchen store."

As they might say in Willmar, meeting Mrs. Olson was a hoot. What I appreciated the most about her was that no-nonsense, Midwestern logic. After all, it's helped her cook at least fifteen thousand meals. I did the math.

You want to talk about a healthy perspective? Check this out:

"My dad was a letter carrier and my mother never worked outside the home, so money was tight.

But I remember meals, when it was time for a paycheck to come, and we'd have oatmeal for supper with ice cream on top, *and we all thought we were kings.*"

When I asked Mrs. Olson for a family recipe she would like me to include in this book, she wanted to point out that *"Any recipe is just sorta the beginning."*

I know that's true, but I don't think I would tinker too much with a recipe from Mrs. Olson. Especially one that was awarded 'runner-up' in an actual, honest-to-goodness Betty Crocker contest. It doesn't get much more real than that.

Mrs. Olson's Piccadillo Chile

Ingredients

1 lb. ground turkey

1/2c sliced green onion

1(4oz) can undrained chopped green chilies

1 clove garlic (minced)

1/2 c raisins

3T almonds

1 1/2 t chili powder

1/2 t cumin

1/2 t cinnamon

1/4 t ground cloves

2 (8oz) cans tomato sauce

1 (14.5 oz.) can whole tomatoes

8 pimento stuffed olives (halved)

Brown meat, stirring and adding onions, chili and garlic. Cook 3 min, add raisins and remaining ingredients. Cover and reduce heat. Simmer at least 15 min.

Everything but the Cranberry

There are only a handful of childhood food memories that have stuck with me. Don't misunderstand, it's not that we didn't eat *well*. But we never ate anything *fancy*.

Even on a fixed income, Mom always made sure we had some meat, some carbs and something green on our plates every evening at five (and to this day, no matter when dinner is supposed to be, I still get hungry around four-thirty).

It's just that dinner was always more *satisfying* than it was *memorable*. For some reason, the only entrée I really remember is her stuffed bell peppers.

I didn't understand cooking, but I thought it was cool that you could take something I didn't like at all (green peppers), and an hour and a half later it would mysteriously taste great.

Another food memory, and one I can almost taste to this day, is of the first fish I ever caught (not that this is relevant, but it also is the only fish I've ever caught).

I was eight years old, and we were camping, and I caught one trout. Cooked it over an open fire next to where I caught it, and to this day, I think it's the best-tasting fish I've ever had.

I also have fond*ish* memories of a food item from the high school cafeteria. It was one of the rotating 'main courses' on the school lunch menu, and it was called a 'Pepper Belly.'

A 'Pepper Belly' was a bag of Fritos corn chips, slit open on the side, covered with chili, cheese and chopped, raw onions. And it was considered a 'main course.'Even in high school, I thought, "This probably isn't the healthiest lunch I could have."

The *strangest* childhood food memories I have involve a pot belly stove. Part of the strangeness is that we *had* a pot belly stove.

For whatever reason, in our seventies-era kitchen, next to the avocado-colored fridge, was a wood-burning stove, like nineteenth-century pioneers would have used.

And we weren't exactly in the wilderness. I grew up in a tract house about ninety miles from Los Angeles.

We mostly used it for heat, but every Christmas morning, I would wake to the ineffable smell of fried eggs and sausage cooking in butter on top of our potbelly stove.

I'm sure we would have been fine with a small space heater, and Mom could have made breakfast on our electric range, but it surely wouldn't have felt like a holiday.

After a couple of years of finding my way around the kitchen, I cooked my first holiday meal last Thanksgiving. In retrospect, I should have chosen an easier holiday (there must be some quick and easy Arbor Day recipes out there).

But I forged ahead, planning to make everything from scratch with one important exception -- the cranberry sauce.

I know there are plenty of recipes for homemade cranberry sauce, but for me, cranberry sauce comes out of a can, shaken onto a plate in one solid mass, still marked by lines from the inside of the can.

I don't care if you slow-roasted your bird for eighteen hours, lovingly mashed each potato by hand, and picked the green beans yourself, if there's not a tube of cranberry 'sauce' on the table, I'll have Thanksgiving dinner somewhere else, thank you very much.

I bought a five pound, bone-in turkey breast, patted it dry, and added a spice rub mix I made, and then I slathered the skin with butter. It's not like we were celebrating National Health Food Day.

The side dishes included homemade mashed potatoes with cumin and roasted Brussels sprouts with a drizzle of lemon juice, a sprinkle of kosher salt and some cracked black pepper.

I made my own dressing, too. I would have made 'stuffing,' but apparently stuffing the bird before you cook it isn't safe anymore, even though people have done it that way for hundreds of years.

Here's where it gets a little weird: some recipes for dressing include eggs, some don't. I opted to go with eggs.

As I've mentioned, I'm not very diligent about measuring things, and after guessing at the 'right' amount of bread and eggs, I could see it was too goopy. Sorta looked like Gerber's.

So, I added more bread. Great -- now it's too dry. More egg, right? And then, at a certain point, I had no more room in my little blender. And my 'dressing' still looked like baby food.

Since I was worried about my turkey, *and* I had no experience with Brussels sprouts, *and* my potatoes were going to be finished way too early, something had to give.

Needing a quick resolution to *the Great Dressing Fiasco of 2011*, I grabbed a meatloaf pan and poured the putative dressing mixture in. Then I shoved it into a toaster oven until I was ready to deal with it.

The reviews of my first holiday meal? The turkey was terrific, the sprouts were spectacular, and the potatoes were . . . well, they were mashed potatoes. Might have been a bit heavy-handed with the cumin.

And as for my transmogrified dressing? Well, it *tasted* like dressing. Or maybe it tasted like stuffing. However, it *looked* more like meatloaf, and you had to *slice* it like a loaf of bread. So on some level, what I ended up doing was taking some bread, and turning it into . . . a different kind of bread.

The most amazing thing about my first Thanksgiving dinner was that, as crazy as the *experience* was, it didn't make *me* crazy. In fact, cooking always makes me feel a little *less* crazy.

I have a feeling Mom would have been proud of my effort. I wish she could have been there to see it. She might have been able to help me with the dressing, but then again, she probably would have just told me to get out of the kitchen while she made it herself.

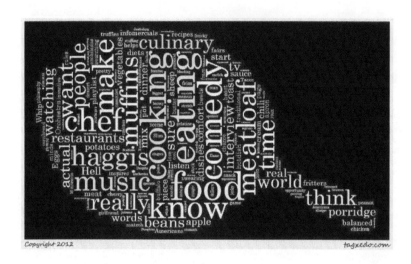

(Not) About the Author

This being my first book, I should probably tell you a bit about who I am. I should, but I think it would be more revealing to tell you who I'm not. So I went soul-searching.

Actually, I went *'ego-surfing,'* which is typing your own name into a search engine to seeing what's been written about you. The great thing about ego-surfing is that it's both pointless *and* self-centered.

And, instead of comparing myself to everyone on the planet (where I would rank somewhere around 3,465,218,107th), I can at least see if I'm one of the most successful people *named 'Michael Dane.'*

In the process, I found a site that gives you statistical information on how your name ranks in popularity, and it tells you where people with your name live.

In fact, there are thirty-three 'Michael Dane' listings in the entire country (making it the 613,590th most popular name), and I/we can be found in twenty states (with five of us in Massachusetts).

A quick search yielded almost ten thousand pages on the internet that have at least one reference to a 'Michael Dane.'

Most of them aren't about me. So, it was time to see how my life's work stacks up against that of the *other* various 'Michael Dane's.

MY RESEARCH STAFF, RESEARCHING THINGS

The first result I found was for a karaoke singer in Spokane, Washington. Seems like a pleasant enough guy in his YouTube videos.

Next, I found a guy in North Carolina who owns his own company, Dane Construction. The only thing noteworthy about this Michael Dane is that federal campaign records show he donated money to *both* candidates in a recent two-person senate race. Pick a side, buddy!

Rounding out the first few, there's a Michael Dane who's listed as a 'voice talent.' But I went to his website, and first of all, he's based in Athens, Texas, which isn't even the hippest Athens in the U.S. His bio says that he was a DJ at a club called 'Toppless,' so we're probably not aiming for the same audience.

There is a link to the MySpace page of a *twenty-one year old girl* in Lorain, Ohio, but I didn't like the looks of her friends. She could do better.

I found an actor with my name, but according to IMDB, his entire resume consists of the roles 'Transvestite Steve' and 'bad guy.' No disrespect, Mike, but neither of the characters you played even had last names.

Also in the world of showbiz, Canadian singer Michael Dane apparently had a minor hit with the 12″ disco single "Let's Make Love" (the flip side, as we all remember, was "The Dead Are Making Love"), but that was in 1981, and I've seen no evidence of a comeback. By him *or* Canadian disco.

The rest of the top 'Michael Dane' results include:

> A Goth kid who takes *far* too many pictures of himself

> A lawyer in Kirtland, Ohio who in 37 years of practice has never had an instance of professional misconduct (and has apparently never left Kirtland, Ohio).

> A man who owns an 'architectural products' company in Phoenix with a sharp-looking website. Curiously, twelve of the sixteen links are 'Under Construction.'

> A guy credited on the album *"A Victorian Christmas For Brass"* who is listed as the 'bell ringer.'

Pretty eclectic group, aren't we? And I think I more than hold my own. Although I do wish I had 'bell ringer' on my resume.

The next contender was fun to read about. An English professor at two colleges in Hawaii, he's listed on ratemyprofessors.com. Here are a few quotes about Professor Dane:

- "Sometimes he seems like he's weird but he's very helpful."
- "He is entertaining to listen to, but jokes can be repetitive."
- "First impression makes Dane seem intimidating. He has a strange sense of humor."

Weird. Those are all really accurate descriptions of *me*. I had to think back, because I wondered for a few minutes whether I had simply forgotten that I had been an English professor in Hawaii. As it turned out, it wasn't me.

My favorite search result referred to a *movie character* named 'Michael Dane,' and from now on, I'm gonna tell people that I was named after him, just to give myself a more interesting backstory.

In the 1923 western "North of Hudson Bay," cowboy star Tom Mix played a rancher named Michael Dane. Sadly, according to the book *'John Ford,'* 'only portions' of the film survive, 'with titles in Czech.' I have no idea why.

Here's a synopsis of the plot:

"Rancher Michael Dane falls in love with Estelle while en route to Northern California where his brother Peter had struck gold. But there he finds his brother dead and his partner MacKenzie sentenced to walk the 'death trail.'

Dane tries to help MacKenzie, earns the same sentence, but both escape, battling wolves, and meet Estelle, pursued by her uncle, the real murderer, who dies after a canoe chase over a waterfall."

It's absolutely uncanny how much that sounds like my life. Just replace 'rancher' with 'writer,' and replace 'battling wolves' with 'writing.' Oh, and instead of a 'canoe chase over a waterfall,' picture me . . . making a meatloaf.

Acknowledgements

All content ©2009-2012 by Michael Dane
Some excerpts previously appeared online at
OpenSalon.com/mistercomedy and MeatloafMuffins.com

All images used are in the public domain, except:

frontispiece, pages 17, 37, 40, 201 **Kara A. Bray**

pages 9, 102, 211 **Michael Dane**

pages 63, 68 **Stan's Doughnuts**

pages 119, 120 **Zoefotografie**

pages 139, 144 **Hell's Kitchen, Minneapolis**

page 23 **Noran Neurological Clinic, Minneapolis**

page 44 **San Gennaro Foods**

page 48 **LandBigFish.com**

page 52 **Weston Supply**

page 73 **Bret's Table (Bret Bannon)**

page 79 **SlapChop.com**

page 93 **Steve Schwab**

page 151 **Frontgage.com**

page 167 **Lynne Rosetto Kasper**

page 184 **BlackGarlic.com**

page 188 **The Cooking Lab, LLC**

page 216 **Rabbi Alan Shavit-Lonstein**

page 222 **Mary Olson**

page 245, back cover **Christopher Grey**

Made in the USA
Charleston, SC
22 June 2012